101 Manifestations of Pride

101
MANIFESTATIONS
of PRIDE

BY

EVANGELIST IMEVBORE ELUGBE

XULON PRESS

Xulon Press
2301 Lucien Way #415
Maitland, FL 32751
407.339.4217
www.xulonpress.com

Paperback ISBN-13: 978-1-6628-4794-3
Ebook ISBN-13: 978-1-6628-4795-0

Dedication

This book is dedicated to my father Prof. Ben Ohi Elugbe
and to my mother
(Rest in Love) Evangelist Stella, Christiana Baiye.

Table of Contents

101 Manifestations of Pride

Introduction

$\mathcal{E}$xodus 20:3 says: **Thou shalt have no other gods before me.** Psalms 82:6 says: **I have said, Ye are gods; and all of you are children of the most High.** Notice in these two scriptures, lower case g is used to spell God and in each scripture it is plural. There are many other gods, many other objects, people, substances etc. that we make into gods. This book is about the first other god (besides the supreme God), which leads to the making of other gods. This god is called the god of self.

Pride also known as idolatry of the self or self-idolatry as one writer puts it. Or as another writer puts it: "it is replacing the grace of God, with demonic ambition." It is the lowest form of love (selfish love), while agape or unconditional love is the highest form of love (selfless love). An idol is anything, place, or person that you have elevated above God. The idol has become more important than God. The idol (whatever it is), now has and controls your exclusive allegiance, which should only belong to God. In todays culture: movie stars, professional athletes, musicians, entertainers, sports teams etc., can and have been made into idols.

This human disease (and the different ways it shows up in our lives), that we all must deal with from time to time is responsible for most of our failed relationships: marital, friendship, conjugal, employee, teammate, church family, neighbor, etc. it is responsible for the ills of society.

Galatians 5:6 says: For in Christ Jesus, neither circumcision nor uncircumcision has any value. The only thing that counts, is faith expressing itself through love (New International Version). According to the latter part of this verse, faith expresses itself through love. In other words, our faith, is fueled by love. The flip side to that is also true i.e., fear (the antithesis of faith) expresses itself through pride. In other words, our fear is fueled by pride.

The Bible tells us that God is love, (1John 4:8). His very nature is love. In the same way, Just as God is love, Satan is pride; his very nature is pride. God does NOT have love, God is love. Satan does NOT have pride, Satan is pride.

There is situational pride, seasonal pride and spiritual pride. We will use King David as our example to explain the difference in the three. David was of a humble spirit at his core. However, there were certain situations where he acted pridefully e.g., when he counted the Israelites (see 1 Chronicles 21). There was also a season in his life where he acted pridefully. The bible talks about the spring season, a time when kings usually went to war, David decided not to go, which eventually led to the Bathsheba incident (see 2 Samuel 11).

There are roughly 3 categories for pride: Vanity, Conceit and Arrogance. Vanity is a fragile form of pride. People's opinions of you can make or break you. Conceit, excessive self-love (very narcissistic, will put others down, to elevate the self). Arrogance is the epitome of pride, no one can tell you anything, if you are good at it and if you are bad at it, its irrelevant.

Whatever, the form of pride, the first line of defense of it is to identify it. Know what it looks like when it shows up. This means we must watch for it, 24 hours of the day, seven days of the week. **1 Peter 5:8 says: Stay alert! Watch out for your great enemy, the devil. He prowls around like a roaring lion looking for someone to devour. (New Living Translation).** How do we watch for the devil; by watching for our prideful ways and its manifestations. We are as holy as we are humble. The litmus test for true holiness is humility. The word human comes from two words: **Hu**mus and man. **Hu**mility is the soil from which all the other virtues (love, joy, patience, peace, kindness, goodness etc) grow (see diagram). **Hu**manity is best expressed in **Hu**mility.

Pride creeps in where its presence is least expected and if we are not on guard, or watching for it, then what has begun in the spirit can be perfected in the flesh! The danger of pride is closer than we think; watch for it.

The 101 listed here are not exhaustive, and I have been guilty of all of them at one point or another. We need the help of the Holy Spirit to overcome our prideful ways. When you recognize a prideful manifestation, repent of it, and God will give you more grace. It is my prayer that this book may help preserve one individual, one family, one community and eventually one nation.

#1

Prayerlessness

2 Chronicles 7:14:

> *if my people, who are called by my name, will*
> *humble themselves and pray and seek my face*
> *and turn from their wicked ways, then I will*
> *hear from heaven, and I will forgive their sin*
> *and will heal their land.*

This verse gives us the connection between humility and prayer. God said: If my people would humble themselves and pray… in other words prayer is a humbling activity. Prayer acknowledges dependence on God. Therefore, if prayer is connected to humility, then the lack thereof is connected to pride. Prayerlessness means independence from God, it says to God, I do not need you. I exist on my own. All of which are not true., but this is what pride does; it deceives us (more on this later).

When we do not pray, we become prey for the enemy. God expects that we His people who are called by His name, if or when we have dishonored His name by our actions, should honor it by accepting the consequences and praying for the removal of the judgment and turning from our evil and wicked

1

ways, and return to God in humility. This return is both on an individual level and on a corporate level

Some have said that this verse does not apply to the church today, but nothing could be further from the truth. Afterall, the church is a spiritual Israel. Romans 2:28-29 says, **[28] After all, who is a real Jew, truly circumcised? It is not the man who is a Jew on the outside, whose circumcision is a physical thing. [29] Rather, the real Jew is the person who is a Jew on the inside, that is, whose heart has been circumcised, and this is the work of God's Spirit, not of the written Law. Such a person receives praise from God, not from human beings** (Good News Translation)

The requirement then, is the same as the requirement now: if we want revival, we must go to God in prayer and repent.

When You Do Not Want to Be Seen Putting Coins in The Offering

Mark 12:41-44:

> *⁴¹ Jesus sat down opposite the place where the offerings were put and watched the crowd putting their money into the temple treasury. Many rich people threw in large amounts. ⁴² But a poor widow came and put in two very small copper coins, worth only a few cents.⁴³ Calling his disciples to him, Jesus said, "Truly I tell you, this poor widow has put more into the treasury than all the others. ⁴⁴ They all gave out of their wealth; but she, out of her poverty, put in everything—all she had to live on."*

One day during service, I sat beside my wife at the time. When it was offering time, I gave her some coins to put in the basket. She refused to put the coins into the basket. I asked her to give me ack the coins so that I could go and put the money in the offering basket. After service, I told her that it was her pride, that did not let her accept the coins. Afterall, just earlier on that same day, I had given her a $20 bill to put in the offering and she took it. She cared what other people would think of her putting coins into the offering; her heart was not right in that giving.

In the story, the widow did not care what anybody thought about her giving; she gave her all. Until we stop caring what other people think or say about us, we cannot give God our all in our time, talent, and treasure. In our worship and in our praise, we will struggle to give God our all if we care what others think and that is a product or a manifestation of our pride. This story shows us that it is not about the amount in giving, it is about the heart. 2 Corinthians 9:7 says: **Every man according as he purposeth in his heart, so let him give; not grudgingly, or of necessity: for God loveth a cheerful giver** (King James Version).

The culture we live in today or even back then would have criticized the widow for giving her last rather than keeping it for herself. However, Christ commended her so her actions were approved of by Christ. Therefore, it did not matter who disapproved of her actions as long as Christ the Savior approved of it.

#3

When told to Come to the altar for prayer regarding a specific need or sin. You know you need it, but you don't want anybody to know

1 Samuel 15:30:

> *Then Saul pleaded again, "I know I have sinned. But please, at least honor me before the elders of my people and before Israel by coming back with me so that I may worship the LORD your God."*

*H*ere again, caring more about what people think than what God thinks and certainly more than being free. The devil dwells in secrecy, and since the devil's very nature is prideful, then the same can be said about the sin of pride. Proverbs 28:13 says: **You will never succeed in life if you try to hide your sins. Confess them and give them up; then God will show mercy to you.** The first Adam (male and Female) sinned, and they immediately went to hide, when they heard the footsteps of God coming towards them. Covering up our sin and hiding our sins, is prideful and it is part of our fallen nature.

In the text, Saul (Israel's first king) cared more about his reputation and how he looked before the people, than displeasing God. He acknowledged that he had sinned but in order to save face, for a show of piety (not sincerity of piety), he asked Samuel to honor him before the people.

#4

Unforgiveness

Matthew 18:32-35:

> *Then the king called in the man he had for-*
> *given and said, 'You evil servant! I forgave*
> *you that tremendous debt because you pleaded*
> *with me.* [33] *Shouldn't you have mercy on your*
> *fellow servant, just as I had mercy on you?'* [34]
> *Then the angry king sent the man to prison to*
> *be tortured until he had paid his entire debt.*
>
> [35] *"That's what my heavenly Father will do to*
> *you if you refuse to forgive your brothers and*
> *sisters[a] from your heart."*

The parable of the unforgiving servant paints a picture of how the pride in our hearts causes us to forget how much we have been forgiven. Our pride causes us to fail to make the connection between how much we have been forgiven and consequently how much we ought to forgive. In other words, no matter how much offense a person commits against you, it pales in comparison to the amount of offense we commit against God.

In the parable, a talent was the highest unit of currency. It was equal to 6,000 days wages of a peasant. 18,000 is the highest single number that can be expressed in the Greek. The unforgiving servant was forgiven the equivalent of 60,000,000 days' worth of wages, but here he was unable to forgive 100 pence (the equivalent of 3 months' worth of wages).

#5

Unrepentance

Luke 18:10-14:

> [10] *"Once there were two men who went up to the Temple to pray: one was a Pharisee, the other a tax collector.* [11] *The Pharisee stood apart by himself and prayed,*[a] *'I thank you, God, that I am not greedy, dishonest, or an adulterer, like everybody else. I thank you that I am not like that tax collector over there.* [12] *I fast two days a week, and I give you one tenth of all my income.'* [13] *But the tax collector stood at a distance and would not even raise his face to heaven, but beat on his breast and said, 'God, have pity on me, a sinner!'* [14] *I tell you,"* said Jesus, *"the tax collector, and not the Pharisee, was in the right with God when he went home. For those who make themselves great will be humbled, and those who humble themselves will be made great* (Good News Translation)

Luke 18:10-14 records a parable told by Jesus about a pharisee and a tax collector or publican as they were sometimes called. In the prayer of the pharisee, he exalted and praised himself; he saw himself as better than others. The scripture says first, he stood apart as if to say you are not in my class, then he also went on to say I am not like everybody else or that tax collector over there. He then went on to justify himself: I fast twice a week etc., notice the Pharisee never repented, or asked for mercy because he did not think he needed it. Afterall, in his mind, he was not like everybody else; he was better. As far as he was concerned, every "t" was crossed and every "i" was dotted and all his ducks were in a row. Pride blinds us towards our own faults and need for repentance because we are too busy looking and scrutinizing the fault of others.

But the tax collector was aware of his plight and his need for mercy, and he went on to repent. Jesus said that it was the tax collector that went home justified and in right standing with God, not the Pharisee. Jesus chose to use a tax collector for the parable, because the Jews saw Jewish tax collectors as the worst of the worst sinners. They were worse than Samaritans, they were traitors, because they overtaxed their fellow countrymen and they worked for the Roman government that was oppressing the Jews.

To repent means to change one's mind about a situation, action etc. it is the Greek word metanoia. For a person to repent, they have to acknowledge that a mistake has been made on their part. This is a difficult thing to do for a person operating under the spirit of pride, because it deals a blow to the ego or to the self. A person operating under the spirit of pride in a given situation, is more in love with the ego than in love with the truth.

Pride is self-exaltation, and self-glorification. When you repent, you are not exalting yourself, but rather lowering yourself or humbling yourself. Thus, for the proud, repenting, apologizing or saying sorry is a difficult thing to do even when they know they are in the wrong. They are too important to repent. Repenting is beneath them.

#6

Shame

Proverbs 11:2:

When pride cometh, then cometh shame: but with the lowly is wisdom. (King James Version)

*A*ccording to Mahtani et al, shame is a negative self-conscious emotion that shows up in the context of negative self-evaluation and undesirable exposure of one's vulnerabilities and shortcomings, and a perceived loss of value in one's eyes as well as others.

According to Proverbs 11:2, shame is a manifestation of pride. Shame is an indication of the presence of pride.

Imagine a potentially embarrassing situation like dropping a food tray in a large gathering such as a student cafeteria. A college student may feel shame for dropping the tray. However, a 5-year-old boy or girl would not feel shame at all. This is because children are humble. They have nothing to be ashamed about. They have no reputation to keep up, unlike the college student that maybe trying to impress a female interest, a fraternal brotherhood etc. Or a two-year-old running naked into a room full of people. The wo year old feels no shame

12

whatsoever, because there is no pride. For an adult however, that's a different story.

Genesis 2:25 says: **And they were both naked, the man and his wife, and were not ashamed.**

Adam and his wife were not ashamed because they had no pride whatsoever. However, after the fall, they were ashamed of their nakedness and went to hide. Hiding is an attempt to prevent shame. Shame is the reward of pride. Just as honor is the reward for humility.

Shame and guilt are two words that people use interchangeably, but there is a slight difference between them. According to the online dictionary, Guilt is a feeling of responsibility or remorse for some offense or crime, whether real or imagined.

Guilt is internal while shame is external. For example, I live alone and if I dropped a tray of food, I would not feel any shame at all, because there is no one else there but me. However, it is possible for me to feel the burden of a wrongdoing, crime or offense while I am all alone at home. For shame to be felt, there has to be the presence of other people otherwise it's probably guilt being felt.

#7

Deception

James 1:22:

But be ye doers of the word, and not hearers only, deceiving your own selves.

*A*ccording to this scripture everybody operates at some level of deception. The only way one is not operating at any level of deception is if one's life is in perfect agreement with the Word of God i.e., you do all the things it tells you to do all the time, and you don't do all the things it tells you not to do all the time. Since no one can make that claim except Jesus, then the areas of our life that are not in alignment with the word, are areas of our deception. The more we do the word the less we are deceived and vice versa.

Now what is the connection between pride and deception? Anytime we go against the Word of God, that is our pride Obadiah 1:3 says this: **the pride of thine heart had deceived thee...** thus my level of pride equals my level of deception.

Deception is failing to acknowledge the truth. we avoid the truth because it threatens our self-esteem or sense of wellbeing. Mike W Martin defines self-deception this way: self-deception is the purposeful or intentional evasion of fully acknowledging something to oneself the more a person engages in self-deception, the more they hinder their ability to discern the truth.

In the words of C. S. Lewis: "there is one vice of which no man in the world is free, which everyone in the world loathes when he sees it in someone else, and which hardly any people except Christians ever imagine that they are guilty of themselves. There is no fault that makes a man more unpopular, no fault which we are more conscious in ourselves. And the more we have it in ourselves, the more we dislike it in others. According to the Christian teachers, the essential vice, the utmost evil, is pride. Unchastity (unfaithfulness), anger, greed, drunkenness, and all that are mere flea bites in comparison. It was through pride that the devil became the devil. Pride leads to every other vice. It is a completely anti-God state of mind,"

#8

Unteachable

Luke 11:1:

And it came to pass, that as he was praying in a certain place, when he ceased, one of his disciples said unto hi Lord, teach us to pray, as John also taught his disciples (**King James Version**)

In this verse, the disciples asked Jesus to teach them how to pray. When you ask someone to teach you something, you are admitting that in this area you are ignorant, and not as knowledgeable as you would like to be. This is a bruise to the ego, and it is very difficult for a person operating in the spirit of pride, who would rather stay quiet and ignorant than reveal their need to be taught.

There is a Chinese proverbial story about a mater and student. Every time the master wanted to tell the student something, the student would say: "oh I already know that." Eventually the master brought a cup of tea to the student and began pouring the tea into the student's cup. The cup began to overflow with the tea, and it was pouring down on the table, the ground and getting on the student. Then the student exclaimed "enough!" to which the master responded "and how do you expect to taste more of my tea if you do not empty your cup"

The student was too full of himself as indicated by the cup of tea of knowledge. He was telling the master; I know all and there is nothing you can teach me. This is a manifestation of pride. He ought to have emptied himself in humility with an open mind, because just as the usefulness of the cup is in its emptiness, we are unable to be used by God, until we empty ourselves, and die to self.

#9

Refusing Correction

Proverbs 12:1:

Any who love knowledge want to be told when they are wrong. It is stupid to hate being corrected. (Good News Translation)

The proud think that they are all that plus the bag of chips. While self-confidence is not a bad thing, there is a thin line between confidence and arrogance. The proud resent and reject anything that will make them come down from their high place. To correct them means they made a mistake. They see themselves as above mistakes. Therefore, rather than admit to a mistake, they may choose to point the blame somewhere else or even to lie, just to avoid any damage to the self or bruise to the ego.

It takes grace to receive correction and God gives grace to the humble. Humiliation is the only ladder to honor in the kingdom of God. The stupid, are the proud who would rather live in a society where their actions go unchecked, and their consciences have been smeared with a hot iron. Those who count as enemies, anyone who tells them the truth, because they love themselves more than they love the truth.

#10

Disobedience

1Kings 13:21-22:

> *And he cried unto the man of God that came from Judah saying, thus Saith the Lord, forasmuch as thou hast disobeyed the mouth of the Lord, and has not kept the commandment which the Lord thy God commandeth thee. But camest back, and hast eaten bread and drunk water in the place, of the which the Lord did say to thee, Eat no bread, and drink no water; thy carcase shall not come unto the sepulchre of thy fathers.* (King James Version)

The bible is full of stories and people who disobeyed God and suffered the consequences even up to destruction. Anytime we go against what God tells us to do, we ae being disobedient and it is our pride that causes us to do that. There is His way of doing things and there is our way of doing things. His way I right and truly is the only way, but because we have been given free-will, we are free to make our own choices, which end up in destruction.

In the story of the text, God specifically told the prophet not to eat bread or water and not to return the same way he came (see verses 1-17). Another old prophet came to him and lied that God spoke to him as well and told him to do exactly opposite of what God told him to do. God is not the author of confusion, neither does he operate like that. The prophet lost his life in terrible fashion due to his disobedience.

#11

Contention

Proverbs 13:10:

Only by pride cometh contention: but with the well advised is wisdom. (King James Version)

According to the online dictionary, contention is strife and opposition. Only means solely, exclusively, alone etc. Whenever and wherever, there is contention, then we can be sure that there is pride involved. The spirit of pride causes one to use ad hominem during arguments.

Ad Hominem is the attacking of an opponent's character or motive rather than answering the argument or claim.

Pride makes men impatient of contradictions, competitions, contempt and even concession. Any slight of the ego is intolerable and unbearable for the proud. Therefore, contentions, quarrels, wars and strife break forth in our families, communities, states, kingdoms and sadly enough, the church. Peace, patience and forgiveness are curse words to the proud: they find such words to be offensive.

#12

Impatience

Ecclesiastes 7:8:

Better is the end of a thing than the beginning thereof: and the patient in spirit is better than the proud in spirit. (King James Version)

*A*ccording to this verse, if to be patient in spirit is better than to be proud in spirit, then it follows that impatience is a manifestation of pride and patience must be connected to humility.

Humble people are patient and will bear long. The patient in spirit will see a project or endeavor through to the end. They will persevere in faith, persevere in cases of contradiction (someone opposes their view), competition (someone sees them as rival), contempt (someone sees them as inferior) or the appearance of anything that slights them or makes them look less important. However, the spirit of pride will cause one to be impatient and not be able to bear long.

#13

Cruelty

1Corinthians 13:4:

Charity suffereth long, and is kind; charity envieth not; charity vaunteth not itself, is not puffed up, (King James Version)

1 Corinthians 13 is a chapter in the bible, famous for love and love's characteristics. However, it can also be a chapter about pride. A simple definition for love is putting others needs above yours. When it comes to pride, you put self needs above the needs of others. Pride is the antithesis of love.

Therefore, if the spirit of love is kind, then the spirit of pride is cruel, inconsiderate, unsympathetic, mean and unkind.

Pride cannot suffer long without being filled with resentment, indignation or revenge motives. Pride will not endure many injuries, or slights.

#14

Keeping Record of Wrong

1 Corinthians 13:5:

love is not ill-mannered or selfish or irritable; love does not keep a record of wrong (Good News Translation)

*P*ride manifests itself in keeping record of wrongs. The only reason why we keep record of wrongs that have been done against us is to use it against the offender again in the future.

For example, people with criminal records have their records from the past used against them in matters of employment, housing etc. keeping record of wrongdoing is closely related to unforgiveness, and both are manifestations of pride.

Psalms 130:3 says **If you kept a record of our sins, who could escape being condemned?** (Good News Translation). According to this scripture, if God kept a record of our wrongdoings and used it against us, we would all be spiritual Felons. None of us can pass a spiritual background check. Therefore, David said I would rather fall into the hands of God than man.

#15

Jealousy

1 Corinthians 13:4:

Love is patient and kind; it is not jealous or conceited or proud; (**Good News Translation**)

Jealousy is the feeling of resentment against someone that is a rival (even though they may not know it). It is resentment against the success of another. However, if we love someone, we will want to see them do good, even better than us. For example, we want our children to do better than we did, because we love them. The spirit of pride manifests itself as jealousy. What God has for you, is for you. There is no need to be jealous of what someone else has. There are several people who do not know what their assignment, purpose, or calling in the earth is. I believe, this has a lot to do with their insecurity. If they knew their assignment, they would not be jealous of anybody else's success.

Jesus was not jealous of John the Baptist success, neither was John jealous of his. Both men knew their purpose and focused on it. They had no time to be jealous, because they were too busy pursuing purpose.

#16

Boasting

Proverbs 27:1-2:

> *Never boast about tomorrow. You don't know*
> *what will happen between now and then.²*
> *Let other people praise you—even strangers;*
> *never do it yourself.* (Good News Translation)

To boast is to speak with excessive pride and exaggeration about oneself. The Hebrew word used here is *halal*. It is one of the seven Hebrew words for praise. It means to shine, to shout, to rave, to celebrate insanely. These are things we should be doing for God. Or saying about God not ourselves. God means self-existing one or self-sufficient one. We are not able to exist on our own. It took the breath of the almighty to give us life. Furthermore, as the scripture says, we do not know what tomorrow will bring, which further proves our dependence on Him.

It was the duty of the Levites under the old covenant to stand every morning and evening to thank and *halal* (praise) the Lord (see 1 Chronicles 23:30). Under the new covenant we have been made priests (Revelations 1:6). We should stand and praise God morning and evening and not boast of ourselves.

James 4:15 says this: **What you should say is this: "If the Lord is willing, we will live and do this or that."** (Good News Translation). This is what we all should be saying. Boasting is not the same as making a faith declaration. A faith declaration is still expressing confidence and reliance on God.

#17

Competition

> [46] *An argument broke out among the disciples as to which one of them was the greatest.* [47] *Jesus knew what they were thinking, so he took a child, stood him by his side,* [48] *and said to them, "Whoever welcomes this child in my name, welcomes me; and whoever welcomes me, also welcomes the one who sent me. For the one who is least among you all is the greatest."* (Good News Translation)

*A*nother manifestation of pride is competition. In this passage of scripture, the disciple asked Christ who the greatest disciple was. They had a contention about it so much so that Christ, who knew their thoughts and wanted to bring peace and unity into the situation, used a child as a symbol of greatness.

There are 9 gifts of the Spirit and 9 fruits of the Spirit. The gifts of the Spirit are the skills and talents we need to get the assignment done here on earth. The fruits of the Spirit are the character qualities of Christ that enable us to dwell together in unity. However, the gifts and callings are without repentance (Romans 11:23). Every believer has a gift but not every believer has fruit. When the gifts are flowing, but the fruits are lacking among believers, then competition and contention, (which are manifestations of pride) are the results. The priestly garment of the Levites was intertwined at the hems with bells and pomegranates. The bells represent the gifts of the Spirit, and the pomegranates represent the fruits of the Spirit.

Imagine a situation where the choir director at a church is feeling threatened by a new member of the congregation, because the new member may be able to sing better. Rather than encourage the new member in their gifting, the choir director decides to bring them down, or talk bad about them etc. the list goes on. Eventually the new member leaves the church in order to avoid strife. Situations like this occur amongst believers and the root cause is the spirit of pride.

#18

Lying

Proverbs 6:16-17:

*These six things doth the LORD hate: yea, seven
are an abomination unto him: A proud look, a
lying tongue, and hands that shed innocent
blood,* (King James Version)

When reading scripture, it is a good practice to pay attention to the order in which things are listed. They are not random or haphazard. Notice in this list, a lying tongue comes right after a proud look. The spirit of pride causes one to tell lies. Here is what Jesus said about Satan, who is the epitome of pride in John 8:44: **Ye are of your father the devil, and the lusts of your father ye will do. He was a murderer from the beginning, and abode not in the truth, because there is no truth in him. When he speaketh a lie, he speaketh of his own: for he is a liar, and the father of it.**

#19

Overvaluing the Praise of Others

John 12:43:

For they loved the praise of men more than the praise of God. (King James Version)

$\mathcal{P}$roverbs 27 and two talks about letting another man praise you and not yourself. However, we must be careful not to keep those praises or glory. We must pass on whatever praise we receive to God. Because only he is worthy to receive glory, honor and power. Revelations 4:12 if we keep the praise that belongs to him then we will soon find ourselves in the situation that John, 12:43 talks about. Loving the praises of men more than the praises of God. Do we care more about what others think than what God thinks? Do we love the Praises of men more than the Praises of God? If the answer is yes, then this is the spirit of pride. If time has shown us anything. It has shown us that we human beings cannot handle glory. The Greek word for glory is doxa. It means weight or importance. Now, you can imagine a person going. To the gym to lift weights. If this person tries to lift a weight that is beyond his or her strength, the person will probably drop the weights on the ground or hurt get hurt. That person must reduce the weight to what he or she can carry or push. So it is with glory; glory is a weight. Most of us cannot handle that weight. And we can only handle little glory at a time if at all. We need to pass that glory on to God.

#20

Overvaluing Self

Romans 12:3:

And because of God's gracious gift to me I say to every one of you: Do not think of yourself more highly than you should. Instead, be modest in your thinking, and judge yourself according to the amount of faith that God has given you. (Good News Translation)

Benjamin Franklin said "if you dine with vanity, you will sup with contempt." We all have strengths and weaknesses. We are not strong in everything, neither are we weak in everything. We must be careful not to think more highly About ourselves, than we ought to just as the scripture says. Just because we are stronger in a particular area than others does not mean we should look down on them or view them with contempt. Because the truth is that others have their areas of strength as well where they are probably stronger than us. So, let's think soberly, moderately or modestly about ourselves.

2 Corinthians 10:18 says: **For it is when the Lord thinks well of us that we are really approved, and not when we think well of ourselves.** (Good News Translation).

21

The Blame Game

Genesis 3:11-13:

> [11] *"Who told you that you were naked?" God asked. "Did you eat the fruit that I told you not to eat?"*[12] *The man answered, "The woman you put here with me gave me the fruit, and I ate it."*[13] *The LORD God asked the woman, "Why did you do this? "She replied, "The snake tricked me into eating it."* (Good News Translation)

We play the blame game to avoid taking responsibility for our actions or to avoid embarrassment or shame. When God asked Adam if he had eaten from the tree, which he had commanded him not to eat from his response was to point the finger at the woman or to blame the woman for his sin. She in turn, blamed the serpent. Keep in mind anytime God asks a question, it is not because he does not know the answer, but rather, He is giving us an opportunity to acknowledge and confess that He is true, and we have been found to be otherwise. The spirit of pride plays the blame game.

#22

Do You Minimize or Trivialize offenses?

1 Samuel 15:13-23:

¹³ As Samuel came close, Saul called out, "GOD's blessings on you! I accomplished GOD's plan to the letter!" ¹⁴ Samuel said, "So what's this I'm hearing—this bleating of sheep, this mooing of cattle?" ¹⁵ "Only some Amalekite loot," said Saul. "The soldiers saved back a few of the choice cattle and sheep to offer up in sacrifice to GOD. But everything else we destroyed under the holy ban." ¹⁶ "Enough!" interrupted Samuel. "Let me tell you what GOD told me last night." Saul said, "Go ahead. Tell me." ¹⁷⁻¹⁹ And Samuel told him. "When you started out in this, you were nothing—and you knew it. Then GOD put you at the head of Israel—made you king over Israel. Then GOD sent you off to do a job for him, ordering you, 'Go and put those sinners, the Amalekites, under a holy ban. Go to war against them until you have totally wiped them out.' So why did you not obey GOD? Why did you grab all this loot? Why, with GOD's eyes on you all the time, did you brazenly carry out this evil?"[20-21] Saul defended himself. "What are you talking about? I did obey GOD. I did the job GOD set for me. I brought in King Agag and destroyed the Amalekites under the terms of the holy ban. So the soldiers saved back a few choice sheep and cattle from the holy ban for sacrifice to GOD at Gilgal—what's wrong with that?"[22-23] Then Samuel said, Do you think all GOD wants are sacrifices—empty rituals just for show? He wants you to listen to him! Plain listening is the thing, not staging a lavish religious production. Not doing what GOD tells you is far worse than fooling around in the occult. Getting self-important around GOD is far worse than making deals with your dead ancestors. Because you said No to GOD's command, he says No to your kingship (The Message Bible)

*I*n general, when it comes to offenses, between human beings, the offender tends to mitigate or minimize the significance or severity of the offense while the victim tends to magnify the significance of it. Both tendencies stem from the spirit of pride. Therefore, under the old covenant, it was said an eye for an eye. Let the punishment fit the crime. However, when it comes to offenses between God and man, that is as serious as it gets. In this passage of scripture, soul has been given the command by God to destroy all the spoils of the war. He decided to keep the best of the sheep and loot, and to spare Agag's life. When confronted by Samuel about the bleating sheep, his response was "only some Amalekite loot.' Saul was trying to minimize the offense to Samuel, but it wasn't about Samuel. It was about God and what He had commanded Saul to do. We will use this same text to discuss another manifestation of pride.

#23

Murmuring/Complaining

Proverbs 14:27:

How long shall I bear with this evil congregation, which murmur against me? I have heard the murmurings of the children of Israel, which they murmur against me.(**King James Version**)

*T*he book of Exodus records several instances of the children of Israel murmuring or complaining against Moses and God. Here also in this passage of scripture in Numbers, we have yet another incident of complaint.

Complaining is a sign of impatience, immaturity and it is a manifestation of pride. complaining speaks of discontentment, but it rarely considers, the totality of the situation or the big picture. The scripture tells us that Godliness with contentment is great gain. Those who complained from 20 years old and up, never got to see the promised land. It was the little ones that inherited the land. One would have expected complaint and murmuring out of the little ones, but it came from the adults. Their murmuring was met with a severe reproof from God.

Nevertheless, He still stayed true to His promise to Abraham by allowing the little ones, who grew up in the wilderness, to inherit the new land. This was made possible through the intercessory prayer of Moses (see Numbers 14:20). The children of Israel complained and murmured after they had seen miracle, after miracle, and provision after provision. They found fault with God and tempted Him. This is the spirit of pride at work.

24

Is it All About You (Me Syndrome)

Jonah 4:1-11:

Jonah was very unhappy about this and became angry. ² So he prayed, "LORD, didn't I say before I left home that this is just what you would do? That's why I did my best to run away to Spain! I knew that you are a loving and merciful God, always patient, always kind, and always ready to change your mind and not punish. ³ Now then, LORD, let me die. I am better off dead than alive."⁴ The LORD answered, "What right do you have to be angry?"⁵ Jonah went out east of the city and sat down. He made a shelter for himself and sat in its shade, waiting to see what would happen to Nineveh. ⁶ Then the LORD God made a plant grow up over Jonah to give him some shade, so that he would be more comfortable. Jonah was extremely pleased with the plant. ⁷ But at dawn the next day, at God's command, a worm attacked the plant, and it died. ⁸ After the sun had risen, God sent a hot east wind, and

> *Jonah was about to faint from the heat of the sun beating down on his head. So he wished he were dead.*[a] *"I am better off dead than alive," he said.*⁹ *But God said to him, "What right do you have to be angry about the plant? "Jonah replied, "I have every right to be angry—angry enough to die!"*¹⁰ *The* LORD *said to him, "This plant grew up in one night and disappeared the next; you didn't do anything for it and you didn't make it grow—yet you feel sorry for it!*¹¹ *How much more, then, should I have pity on Nineveh, that great city. After all, it has more than 120,000 innocent children in it, as well as many animals!"* (Good News Translation)

*A*s mentioned earlier Pride is self-idolatry. It's all about the self and selfish desires. Nineveh had oppressed Israel for a long time and so there was a hatred and enmity between. Israel and Nineveh. Nineveh was the capital of Assyria. In this text, Jonah is extremely angry that the Lord was going to have mercy on Nineveh even though it was because of his preaching. Jonah was so focused on himself; he had more compassion for a gourd (The plant that was providing shade for him) than for a whole nation of ignorant people. If his heart was in the right place, he should have been rejoicing, that a whole nation repented and turned to God at his preaching. The Bible says heaven rejoices for every for one Soul that repents. But he was hung up on the pain that the city of Nineveh had caused Israel in the past, and all he wanted was retribution. He wanted nothing good to go their way. However, we just like Jonah, must understand that it's never about our will being done. It's always about His will being done. (see Matthew 6:11)

#25

Holding on to the Victim Role

Matthew 18:21-35:

²¹ Then Peter came to Jesus and asked, "Lord, if my brother keeps on sinning against me, how many times do I have to forgive him? Seven times?"²² "No, not seven times," answered Jesus, "but seventy times seven,[a] ²³ because the Kingdom of heaven is like this. Once there was a king who decided to check on his servants' accounts. ²⁴ He had just begun to do so when one of them was brought in who owed him millions of dollars. ²⁵ The servant did not have enough to pay his debt, so the king ordered him to be sold as a slave, with his wife and his children and all that he had, in order to pay the debt. ²⁶ The servant fell on his knees before the king. 'Be patient with me,' he begged, 'and I will pay you everything!' ²⁷ The king felt sorry for him, so he forgave him the debt and let him go.²⁸ "Then the man went out and met one of his fellow servants who owed him a few dollars.

He grabbed him and started choking him. 'Pay back what you owe me!' he said. [29] His fellow servant fell down and begged him, 'Be patient with me, and I will pay you back!' [30] But he refused; instead, he had him thrown into jail until he should pay the debt. [31] When the other servants saw what had happened, they were very upset and went to the king and told him everything. [32] So he called the servant in. 'You worthless slave!' he said. 'I forgave you the whole amount you owed me, just because you asked me to. [33] You should have had mercy on your fellow servant, just as I had mercy on you.' [34] The king was very angry, and he sent the servant to jail to be punished until he should pay back the whole amount."[35] And Jesus concluded, "That is how my Father in heaven will treat every one of you unless you forgive your brother from your heart." (Good News Translation).

We hold on to the victim role in a variety of ways. For example, when we want people to feel sorry for us, or when we want attention. However, unforgiveness is tied to holding on to the victim role as in the parable of the unforgiving servant in our text. This is a manifestation of pride.

The victim role gives us a sense of power: "I have something on you that I can use against you." However, when we hold on to the victim stance, we let go of the victory stance. The Victim stance gives us "control" but when we put things in perspective (looking at the big picture), we hopefully soon realize that God is truly the one in control not us. So we can then give up whatever control or power we think we have over the offender.

As in the parable, the king represents God who was truly in control. The unforgiving servant thought he was in control when he was choking his fellow servant.

#26

Do You Think in Perspective or Distortion?

Matthew 25:1-13:

"At that time the Kingdom of heaven will be like this. Once there were ten young women who took their oil lamps and went out to meet the bridegroom. [2] Five of them were foolish, and the other five were wise. [3] The foolish ones took their lamps but did not take any extra oil with them, [4] while the wise ones took containers full of oil for their lamps. [5] The bridegroom was late in coming, so they began to nod and fall asleep.[6] "It was already midnight when the cry rang out, 'Here is the bridegroom! Come and meet him!' [7] The ten young women woke up and trimmed their lamps. [8] Then the foolish ones said to the wise ones, 'Let us have some of your oil, because our lamps are going out.' [9] 'No, indeed,' the wise ones answered, 'there is not enough for you and for us. Go to the

store and buy some for yourselves.' [10] *So the*
foolish ones went off to buy some oil; and
while they were gone, the bridegroom arrived.
The five who were ready went in with him to
the wedding feast, and the door was closed.[11]
"Later the others arrived. 'Sir, sir! Let us in!'
they cried out. [12] *'Certainly not! I don't know*
you,' the bridegroom answered."[13] *And Jesus*
concluded, "Watch out, then, because you do
not know the day or the hour. (Good News
Translation)

*A*ccording to the online dictionary, distorted means not
truly or completely representing the facts or reality.
Distortion then is a lie, and lies have their roots in pride,

Because of delayed consequences, we may not be putting
things in perspective. In other words, our thoughts become distorted. Something called the "distant elephant." At 300 yards,
an elephant looks small. However, the closer it gets, the bigger
it gets. Oftentimes, because consequences seem far off and
we're not thinking ahead or in perspective of the future, we may
act impulsively time and time again, until that elephant that was
far away is now right in front of our face and its towering presence is overwhelming and seems insurmountable. The distant
elephant represents delayed consequences. In our text, the five
wise virgins thought wisely. They took their lamps, saved their
oil until it was time for the bridegroom to come, the five foolish
virgins only thought of the now. Notice the bridegroom came
at midnight. The distant elephant shows up at the most inop-
portune times. The delayed consequences will show up at the
most inconvenient time. Proverbs 11:2, equates wisdom with

the humble. The opposite of wisdom is foolishness. And so, if wisdom is with the humble, then these five foolish virgins were operating in the spirit of pride. They could not bear long. They could not be patient and wait for the groom. They only thought of themselves. and lived for the now.

#27

Are You in Denial

Matthew 26:69-75:

[69] *Peter was sitting outside in the courtyard when one of the High Priest's servant women came to him and said, "You, too, were with Jesus of Galilee."* [70] *But he denied it in front of them all. "I don't know what you are talking about," he answered,* [71] *and went on out to the entrance of the courtyard. Another servant woman saw him and said to the men there, "He was with Jesus of Nazareth."* [72] *Again Peter denied it and answered, "I swear that I don't know that man!"* [73] *After a little while the men standing there came to Peter. "Of course you are one of them," they said. "After all, the way you speak gives you away!"* [74] *Then Peter said, "I swear that I am telling the truth! May God punish me if I am not! I do not know that man!" Just then a rooster crowed,* [75] *and Peter remembered what Jesus had told him: "Before the rooster crows, you will say three times that*

you do not know me." He went out and wept bitterly. (Good News Translation)

*P*sychology defines denial as when a person cannot or will not accept an unpleasant truth.

In our text, the unpleasant truth was that Just as Jesus had previously told Peter what he would do, he was now doing. Jesus had previously told Peter that before the rooster crows once, he would have denied him thrice. Denial is a form of deception, and our level of deception equals our level of pride.

Peter refused to face the facts because at that point denying made his life easier, perhaps saving his skin but when the cock crowed the third time and he remembered Christ words to him (see Luke 22:59-62) and Christ turned and looked straight at him. He wept bitterly and had it not been the prayers of Christ for him, he may never have recovered from the burden of guilt.

#28

Universals

1Kings 19:10:

> *¹⁰ He answered, "L*ORD *God Almighty, I have always served you—you alone. But the people of Israel have broken their covenant with you, torn down your altars, and killed all your prophets. I am the only one left—and they are trying to kill me!"* (Good News Translation)

Statements like "I know everything" or "I am always right" are called universal statements. We need to be careful making such statements because they are generally not true. The prophets in the Old Testament were an endangered species during the time of the prophet Elijah. However, the prophet Elijah made a universal statement. He said to the Lord, "I am the only prophet left" "I have always served you." This led to the Lord replacing him with the prophet Elisha. God always keeps a remnant, but the prophet was focusing on himself, over-valuing himself, and thinking he was indispensable. This was situational pride by the prophet Elijah.

#29

Assumptions and Presumptions

2 Kings 3:26-29:

> *²¹ Abner told David, "I will go now and win all Israel over to Your Majesty. They will accept you as king, and then you will get what you have wanted and will rule over the whole land." David gave Abner a guarantee of safety and sent him on his way. ²² Later on Joab and David's other officials returned from a raid, bringing a large amount of loot with them. Abner, however, was no longer there at Hebron with David, because David had sent him away with a guarantee of safety. ²³ When Joab and his men arrived, he was told that Abner had come to King David and had been sent away with a guarantee of safety. ²⁴ So Joab went to the king and said to him, "What have you done? Abner came to you—why did you let him go like that? ²⁵ He came here to deceive you and to find out everything you do and everywhere you go. Surely you know that!"²⁶*

*After leaving David, Joab sent messengers to get Abner, and they brought him back from Sirah Well; but David knew nothing about it. ²⁷ When Abner arrived in Hebron, Joab took him aside at the gate, as though he wanted to speak privately with him, and there he stabbed him in the stomach. And so Abner was murdered because he had killed Joab's brother Asahel. ²⁸ When David heard the news, he said, "The L*ORD* knows that my subjects and I are completely innocent of the murder of Abner. ²⁹ May the punishment for it fall on Joab and all his family! In every generation may there be some man in his family who has gonorrhea or a dreaded skin disease or is fit only to do a woman's work or is killed in battle or doesn't have enough to eat!"* (Good News Translation)

When you make assumptions, you take things for granted and when you take things for granted, you do things presumptuously or things you have no right to do.

Abner killed Joab's brother in battle and Joab wanted revenge on Abner. While Joab was away, Abner came and made a covenant with David. When Joab came back, and he heard that Abner came, he assumed he knew why Abner came and what was going on. He erroneously thought that Abner came to find out David's activities. His assumption was the pretext he used to presumptuously go after Abner and kill him, which was the true intent in his heart. However, he did not tell David, because he knew he had no right to do that.

#30

Sowing Discord

Proverbs 6:16-19:

*^{16} These six things doth the L*ORD *hate: yea, seven are an abomination unto him:^{17} A proud look, a lying tongue, and hands that shed innocent blood,^{18} An heart that deviseth wicked imaginations, feet that be swift in running to mischief,^{19} A false witness that speaketh lies, and he that soweth discord among brethren.*
(King James Version)

$\mathcal{T}$he spirit of pride manifests itself as stirring up strife between others. Where one should be mediating a situation, they are meddling, causing trouble, sowing discord as the King James version puts it. Proverbs 29:11 says **A fool uttereth all his mind: but a wise man keepeth it in till afterwards.** (King James Version). Not everything that comes to our mind are we to speak, especially in situations where we know that if we reveal such information to either of the parties involved, it will cause more disunity.

#31

Envy

1 Corinthians *13:4:*

> *⁴ Charity suffereth long, and is kind; charity envieth not; charity vaunteth not itself, is not puffed up,* (King James Version)

*A*nother word for envy is covetousness, which the bible calls greed, which is idolatry. The bible does tell us to covet earnestly (not enviously) the best spiritual gifts (see 1 Corinthians 12:31), but the envy here is the envy of another's worldly possessions, which makes it bitter and hostile in nature (see James 3:14).

Envy is closely connected to emulations, which is connected to rivalry and competition, which are manifestations of pride.

#32

Dishonor

Proverbs 18:12:

*Before destruction the heart of man is haughty,
and before honour is humility.*

(King James Version)

This verse connects honor to humility, which means pride is connected to dishonor. Another word for dishonor is disrespect. To dishonor a person is to destroy their reputation. It is to behave in a way or talk in a way that brings shame or reproach on them. Pride is the antithesis of love. When Jesus was asked which commandment was the greatest commandment (see Matthew 22:36-40), He said love for God is connected love for neighbor. However, the spirit of pride does not love the neighbor as the self, but rather pride loves the ego more than the neighbor and more than God.

American politics is rife with dishonor. As each candidate is trying to destroy the other candidate's reputation. In the presidential debate between Donald Trump and Hillary Clinton, the dishonor during the debate was so terrible that one reporter had to ask if they could find something good to say about each other.

Exodus 20:12 says **Honour thy father and thy mother: that thy days may be long upon the land which the LORD thy God giveth thee.** (King James Version). It does not qualify what type of parents you had. Whether your parents were never there or were always there, there is no qualification. It just says to honor them. Children now adays dishonor parents because they were not there for them either because they were incarcerated or hooked on drugs etc., but whatever the reason, God still expects us to respect our parents because those were the vessels He chose to use to bring us into the earth.

#33

Self-Seeking

1 Corinthians 13:5:

> *Doth not behave itself unseemly, seeketh not her own, is not easily provoked, thinketh no evil* (King James Version)

Phillipians 2:3-4:

> *³ Don't do anything from selfish ambition or from a cheap desire to boast, but be humble toward one another, always considering others better than yourselves. ⁴ And look out for one another's interests, not just for your own.* (Good News Translation)

A gain, love puts the interests, benefits and needs of others above the self. Pride does the exact opposite: it puts the benefits, needs and interests of the self above others. The spirit of pride only seeks for the self, and it is not concerned about others. There is no greater enemy or threat to Christian love than the spirit of pride. We must love our neighbor as ourselves. We must rejoice in our neighbor's prosperity as if it were our own and mourn with those that mourn. I am my neighbor, and my neighbor is me. We must make his case our own, not as busybodies or gossipers meddling in the affairs of others, but rather with sympathy and discretion.

#34

Quick to Anger

Ecclesiastes 7:9:

Be not hasty in thy spirit to be angry: for anger resteth in the bosom of fools.

(King James Version)

The opposite of wisdom is foolishness. According to Proverbs 11:2, wisdom is with the humble, which means foolishness must be with the proud.

The anger that scripture talks about here is not righteous indignation, but the type of anger that has a malicious intent. The Lord is slow to anger and quick to mercy, but for most of us we are quick to anger and slow to mercy. If you are quick to anger, be quick to resolve it as well. Ephesians 4:26 says **Be ye angry, and sin not: let not the sun go down upon your wrath:** (King James Version). The longer one stays angry the harder it becomes to stop being angry.

35

Do you Major in the Minor and Minor in the Major?

Matthew 23:24:

Blind guides! You strain a fly out of your drink, but swallow a camel! (Good News Translation)

*A*nother way the spirit of pride manifests itself is when people focus more on less important things to the neglect of the more important things. Jesus was not meaning that the Pharisees did this literally, but the idea is that the Pharisees focused and scrutinized the little stuff while neglecting the big stuff.

In Matthew 7:3-5, Jesus said **³ Why, then, do you look at the speck in your brother's eye and pay no attention to the log in your own eye? ⁴ How dare you say to your brother, 'Please, let me take that speck out of your eye,' when you have a log in your own eye? ⁵ You hypocrite! First take the log out of your own eye, and then you will be able to see clearly to take the speck out of your brother's eye** (Good News Translation). The log in one's eye is more important than the speck in the neighbor's eye. We are to magnify our own fault over our neighbors. We are to major in our own faults and minor in our neighbors.

However, the spirit of pride does the exact opposite. It focuses on others fault to the neglect of self. When people start nitpicking, that's a sure sign they have neglected the more important stuff (their major fault) to focus on their neighbors less important stuff (minor faults). This is a sure manifestation of pride.

#36

Do you Rejoice with the Truth

1 Corinthians 13:6*:*

Rejoiceth not in iniquity, but rejoiceth in the truth; (King James Version).

*L*ove is not happy with evil but is happy with the truth another translation says. The spirit of pride loves self more than the truth. So rather than be happy with the truth, the spirit of pride is happy with deception. Love takes no pleasure in doing harm to anyone even to enemies, but the spirit of pride does. It does not rejoice at the failure of others. This is important when it comes to group dynamics or team sports or any type of body of individuals working together. One person's failure is everybody's failure because you are all affected by it. It is demonic to be delighted at the misery of failure of another.

Love rejoices in the truth of the gospel i.e., the success of it. To see men being changed from glory to glory by it.

#37

False Witnessing

Exodus 23:1:

"Do not spread false rumors, and do not help a guilty person by giving false testimony. (Good News Translation)

False witnesses, falsehood, anything false is a lie and this is a manifestation of the spirit of pride. Keeping quiet while you know the truth and you allow the false rumors to spread is cosigning with the false witness. You are just as guilty as the one spreading the rumors.

#38

Condemnation

Proverbs 3:3:

Let not mercy and truth forsake thee: bind them about thy neck; write them upon the table of thine heart: (King James Version)

Truth is the reason for mercy. When people struggle with being merciful, it is because they are not being truthful. If they would be truthful, they would be merciful. I need to be merciful to my brothers and sisters because the truth is sometimes, I need mercy too. So, if truth is the reason for mercy, then deception is the reason for condemnation. Because deception is the antithesis of truth just as condemnation is the antithesis of mercy. And we already know from Obadiah 1:3 that our level of pride is equal to our level of deception. Therefore, the spirit of pride manifests itself as condemnation.

#39

Preaching without Practicing

Matthew 23:3*:*

So you must obey and follow everything they tell you to do; do not, however, imitate their actions, because they don't practice what they preach. (Good News Translation)

The Pharisees and Scribes were expounders of the Mosaic law. However, they were hypocrites in that they were not practicing what they were preaching. This is a serious manifestation of pride. However, Christ in His divine wisdom told His disciples to obey and follow everything they told them to do. In other words, we must not think the worst of good truths even though they are preached by bad ministers. The truth is the truth even if it is coming out of devil's mouth. We would prefer that our teachers and preachers practiced what they were preaching but if that is who God is using at the time to bring you the bread of life then take it and thank Him for it. Solomon was the wisest man who ever lived, but he did not always practice what he preached in the proverbs. Nevertheless, we still refer to his proverbs constantly.

#40

Putting Burdens on Others

Matthew 23:4:

> *For they bind heavy burdens and grievous to be borne, and lay them on men's shoulders; but they themselves will not move them with one of their fingers.* (King James Version)

Contextual. Jesus was talking about the burden of the law as explained by the scribes and Pharisees. But it is still applicable here as it relates to unforgiveness. Love bears the burdens of others. Love suffers for others. When we forgive, we take on the additional burden of the offender. Pride on the other hand, places additional burden on the offender. So placing heavy burdens on people shoulders, but themselves not being willing to help lift the burden is a picture of unforgiveness and a manifestation of pride.

#41

The Show

Matthew 23:5:

But all their works they do for to be seen of men: they make broad their phylacteries, and enlarge the borders of their garments,

(King James Version)

Is everything you do for the purpose of being seen by people? This spirit of pride is more concerned with looking good or seeming good than being good. The Pharisees had a show of piety, but not a sincerity of piety. The Pharisees pretended the purposes of God, but really intended the purposes of self. The phylacteries where the boxes they wore on their forehead and arm, which contained scriptures. In Numbers 15:38, God told the children of Israel to make borders of fringes on their garments to distinguish them from other nations. However, the Pharisees were not content to have the fringes like others, theirs must be different. They made them noticeable for people to see. They fasted for people to notice, and they prayed for people to notice. The Pharisees who were a picture of pride were all about the show. Pride is all about the show.

We are to let our light so shine that men may see our good works and glorify the Father in heaven (see Matthew 5:15-16) not glorify us. Pride is more interested in the form of Godliness but not the power of it.

#42

Do You Love Places of Honor

Luke 14:10-11.

> *¹⁰ But when thou art bidden, go and sit down in the lowest room; that when he that bade thee cometh, he may say unto thee, Friend, go up higher: then shalt thou have worship in the presence of them that sit at meat with thee.¹¹ For whosoever exalteth himself shall be abased; and he that humbleth himself shall be exalted.* (King James Version)

We have seen. That pride loves to dishonor others and their reputation. Conversely, pride loves places of honor for the self. In this passage of scripture, Jesus is teaching us to humble ourselves by taking the lower seat. It is better for us to be called up than for us to be told to get down. It takes someone with a realistic perspective of their self to do that. Humility is not synonymous with low self-esteem. Neither is it a sign of weakness as the world tends to think. It takes the strong to forgive. It takes the strong to admit wrong and apologize.

#43

Withholding Information
In Order to Maintain Control

Matthew 23:13:

"How terrible for you, teachers of the Law and
Pharisees! You hypocrites! You lock the door
to the Kingdom of heaven in people's faces,
but you yourselves don't go in, nor do you
allow in those who are trying to enter!
(Good News Translation)

*I*n the Old Testament, the Spirit of the Lord had not yet
been poured out on all flesh. The teachers of the law, were
responsible for giving information, breaking down scripture
and imparting understanding to the children of Israel. However,
in their hypocrisy (because they did not practice what they
preached), they would withhold the key of knowledge from the
people, in order to maintain control or superiority over them.
They withheld the key of knowledge in order to keep people
from believing in Christ the Messiah. They had the knowledge
of the Old Testament scriptures enough to open the eyes of the

understanding of the people to see Christ. They, however, did not. Meekness is power under control, but pride corrupts power. It has been said that absolute power corrupts absolutely. I disagree with this statement, because if absolute power corrupts, then our Lord and Savior Jesus the Christ should be corrupt, (but He is not). After all, He said in Matthew 28:18 that all power had been given unto Him in Heaven and in earth. That is as absolute as it gets when it comes to power, yet He was not corrupt. It is not absolute power that corrupts, it is pride that corrupts power. Meekness is power under control. God called Moses the meekest man on the earth. Power itself is not a bad thing, it must be used responsibly. Similarly, money itself is not the root of evil, but the love of it is what scripture calls the root of all evil (see 1 Timothy 6:10)

#44

Do You Hold Others to Standards that you Do Not Keep?

Matthew 23:4:

> *They tie onto people's backs loads that are heavy and hard to carry, yet they aren't willing even to lift a finger to help them carry those loads.* (Good News Translation)

*I*n this text, we see that the Pharisees placed burdens on the people, and they were not willing to help them lift the burden. The Pharisees held the people to standards, they themselves did not keep or help the people keep. They in some cases, interpreted the law in a way that was a benefit to them, but a burden to the people, and if the people. fell short of their standard, their traditions, then they were blamed, and it was their fault. This is the spirit of pride at work.

#45

Stubbornness /
Unwillingness to Change

1 Samuel 15:23:

> *For rebellion is as the sin of witchcraft, and stubbornness is as iniquity and idolatry. Because thou hast rejected the word of the LORD, he hath also rejected thee from being king.* (King James Version)

Someone who is stubborn is unwilling to change their mind even considering evidence of the need to do so. When it comes to the commandments of God, and obedience to them, one need not be stubbornly disobedient (as in the case of Saul in the text), because that is the spirit of pride. As mentioned earlier, anytime we go against God and His word, that is the spirit of pride.

We should be stubbornly obedient to the commandments of God. Just like it says in Isaiah 50:7: **For the Lord God will help me; therefore shall I not e confounded: therefore have I set my face like a flint and I know that I shall not be ashamed** (King James Version).

#46

Do You Condemn Publicly What You Practice Privately?

Genesis 38:24-26:

> *[24] And it came to pass about three months after, that it was told Judah, saying, Tamar thy daughter in law hath played the harlot; and also, behold, she is with child by whoredom. And Judah said, Bring her forth, and let her be burnt.[25] When she was brought forth, she sent to her father in law, saying, By the man, whose these are, am I with child: and she said, Discern, I pray thee, whose are these, the signet, and bracelets, and staff.[26] And Judah acknowledged them, and said, She hath been more righteous than I; because that I gave her not to Shelah my son. And he knew her again no more.* (King James Version)

Judah had 3 sons. The first one, the bible records was wicked in the sight of the Lord and so the Lord slew him. The second one went into his dead brother's wife as their culture required, but because the child would not be seen as his but his brother's, so he coitus interruptus. This was very displeasing in the sight of the Lor and so the Lord slew him.

The third son was not yet grown enough to become Tamar's husband so Judah told his daughter in-law to remain a widow until the third son (Shelah) was old enough to be her husband. However, when Shelah was old enough, Judah still did not offer his son to her as he said he would (for obvious reasons: probably fear that he too may die, or perhaps he thought she was cursed).

Tamar came into the knowledge of this and disguised herself as a harlot. One day while Judah was passing by, he had sex with her and pledged her a young goat and she kept his signet ring as well as his staff till he would bring the pledge. When Judah sent one of his servants with the pledge, Tamar was not there, and upon inquiry about the harlot that sat there, they said there was no such harlot. Tamar conceived by him and after 3 months she was found to be pregnant. Judah's first words when he found out that Tamar was pregnant were: "bring her forth and let her be burnt." Then he found out that it was with him she had played the harlot when she showed him his staff and ring. At least he acknowledged then that she had been more righteous than he was in the matter. He was going to have Tamar condemned to be burned. This is the spirit of pride at work. **We are not better than the people we condemn.**

#47

Do You Think You Are Above Mistakes?

Matthew 26:33:

Peter answered and said unto him, Though all men shall be offended because of thee, yet will I never be offended. (King James Version)

$\mathcal{P}$eter thought he was above mistakes when he declared to our Lord and savior that even if all else failed, he would never fail. However, we know what happened a few verses later. We are all imperfect beings. Sometimes we will miss the mark, we will fall short, and we will drop the ball. If we lose sight of this, then the spirit of pride has crept in. No one is above mistakes. This is important because when it comes to self-forgiveness, we will struggle in that area and find it difficult to forgive ourselves more such actions or inactions.

#48

Do you Think you are Better than Others?

Phillipians 2:3:

Don't do anything from selfish ambition or from a cheap desire to boast, but be humble toward one another, always considering others better than yourselves.

(Good News Translation)

The spirit of pride thinks of the self as better than others or above others. Therefore, certain menial tasks are considered beneath the self, and would rather take a back seat and let other "less important" people do those tasks.

#49

Giving God Ultimatums (Making Demands)

1 Samuel 8:19-22:

> *¹⁹ Nevertheless the people refused to obey the voice of Samuel; and they said, Nay; but we will have a king over us;²⁰ That we also may be like all the nations; and that our king may judge us, and go out before us, and fight our battles.²¹ And Samuel heard all the words of the people, and he rehearsed them in the ears of the LORD.²² And the LORD said to Samuel, Hearken unto their voice, and make them a king. And Samuel said unto the men of Israel, Go ye every man unto his city.* (King James Version)

The children of Israel demanded for a king because Samuel's sons did not have the same integrity as their father: they took bribes and perverted justice in their judgment. They demanded for a king even after Samuel had told them the implications of what they were asking for. (see verses 10-18)

Furthermore, their tone was one of an ultimatum. If they were not gratified in their demand, they would either rise in rebellion against Samuel or defect from their religion completely to serve other gods. This is the spirit of pride at work.

#50

Do you care about the title more than the task? (Executive Christian)

Matthew 23:7:

And greetings in the markets, and to be called of men Rabbi, Rabbi, (King James Version)

The Pharisees loved for their ego to be stroked. They loved to be called Rabbi, which literally means (my great one). However, the same Pharisees placed burdens on the people that they were not willing to lift themselves. They loved to be served rather than to serve. This is a clear manifestation of pride.

My pastor often uses the term executive Christian to refer to preachers who wear 3 piece suits, but are too important to take out the trash at the place of worship. They care more about the title than the task or he function. This is the spirit of pride.

#51

Self-Justification

Luke 10:29:

*But he, willing to justify himself, said unto
Jesus, And who is my neighbour?*

(King James Version)

*I*n this scripture, the expert in the law of Moses wanted to be right. He wanted to have the last word in the discussion. Self-justification is a manifestation of pride. The Pharisees and scribes who were pictures of pride, always sought to justify themselves before men. In Luke 16:15, Jesus said to the Pharisees, ye are they which justify yourselves before men, But God knoweth, your heart, for the highly esteemed among men, is an abomination in the sight of God.

When Saul's sin was brought to him, rather than immediately acknowledge wrongdoing, he chose to justify or defend himself. "I did obey God." I did the job God told me to do. It wasn't until verse 24 that he finally acknowledged wrongdoing (see 1Samuel 15:19-24). And when he acknowledged wrongdoing, which is a place of humility, then the truth came out. He cared more about pleasing. his men or the people. Now it is possible to compare Saul's reaction when confronted with his sin by the prophet Samuel with David's reaction when confronted with his sin by the prophet Nathan. Saul reacted by immediately defending himself, but David reacted by immediately confessing and repenting. It has been said that actions speak louder than words. However, reactions speak louder than actions about a person's disposition or character. So, we can see from the reactions of both kings why God said of David. He is a man after my own heart, but of Saul, He said, I regret that I made him king.

#52

Are you able to put yourself in your neighbors Shoes?

Matthew 7:12:

> *Therefore all things whatsoever ye would that*
> *men should do to you, do ye even so to them:*
> *for this is the law and the prophets.*
>
> (King James Version)

Therefore, is a transitional word that implies a cause-and-effect relationship. Whatever was said before is the cause and what is said after is the effect. As we look at the previous verses, Jesus was talking about asking and receiving, and He said things like if your son asked you for a loaf of bread, would you give him a stone. He also went on to say if we being evil know how to give good things, then how much more our heavenly father (verse 11). That was the cause, and the effect is verse 12, which basically says we should do unto others as you would have them to do unto you.

For me to do that, I must be able to put myself in my neighbors' shoes and ask the question: if this were me, how would

I want to be treated? After I answer the question, then I take the initiative and treat my neighbor the way I would like to be treated. However, the spirit of pride says, "I will never be caught doing that" or "I could never be in that position" or "it could never happen to me" especially when it comes to situations where the action is rather demeaning or frowned at by society.

#53

Do you get mad if you are not given the credit or if you are acknowledged less?

1Samuel 18:6-9:

> *⁶ As David was returning after killing Goliath and as the soldiers were coming back home, women from every town in Israel came out to meet King Saul. They were singing joyful songs, dancing, and playing tambourines and lyres. ⁷ In their celebration the women sang, "Saul has killed thousands, but David tens of thousands." ⁸ Saul did not like this, and he became very angry. He said, "For David they claim tens of thousands, but only thousands for me. They will be making him king next!*
> **(Good News Translation)**

*G*oliath the Philistine had mocked Israel for 40 days. No one had the courage to fight him. The King even offered huge rewards for anyone with the courage to fight and defeat the giant. David rose to the challenge, and we know how the story ended with David being victorious. Now all of Israel is happy and the women are singing, but there is one problem: The women are giving more credit to David than Saul and Saul in his pride cannot accept this.

It is nice to hear one's name mentioned or receive credit for work done, but that should not be your motivation, because if your main motivation is to hear your name mentioned, then that is prideful. Here is a question to ponder: if it were the other way around, and the women were giving more credit to Saul, do you think David would have reacted the same way?

#54

Do you want to teach others but never want to learn from them?

Colossians 3:16:

> *Christ's message in all its richness must live in your hearts. Teach and instruct one another with all wisdom. Sing psalms, hymns, and sacred songs; sing to God with thanksgiving in your hearts.* (Good News Translation)

*A*s the Sunday school superintendent at a small local church, it was my responsibility to set the teaching schedule, which was set to a rotational schedule. In a typical month, each teacher would teach one Sunday and be taught 3 Sundays, before it was their turn to teach again.

I noticed however, that there was this guy who only came on the Sundays he was to teach, and he would leave afterwards. I said something to the Pastor about it. The Pastor said "maybe he works on Sundays. I said "maybe, but it doesn't seem to affect the Sundays he has to teach." So, the Pastor said he would say something to him and sure enough from that point on, he started coming on Sundays he was not teaching. It was not because he had a Sunday job, it was simply his pride and ego telling him we needed to hear from him, but he didn't need to hear from us because there was nothing, we could teach him that he didn't already know.

#55

Don't tell me what to do!

Matthew 23:3a:

So you must obey and follow everything they tell you to do; (Good News Translation)

A wise man once said: "as long as we live, we will always be told what to do by some authority." This is so true. Whether it is our parents at home, or teachers at school or supervisors on the job or the state and federal government agencies, we will be told what to do.

According to this text, Jesus says we must obey the recognized authorities put in place over us. It is the spirit of pride that manifests itself as disobedience to authorities. However, there are two specific cases to address where disobedience maybe warranted. The first is when the authorities in place are unfair and oppressive in nature, and the second is when there are too many chiefs and not enough Indians.

In the former case, it can lead to civil disobedience or an insurrection for example, the civil rights movement because ultimately, the authorities in place are in disobedience to God and His commandments. A civil disobedience is the refusal to obey certain laws or governmental demands for the purpose of influencing legislation or government policy, characterized by the employment of such nonviolent techniques as boycotting, picketing and nonpayment of taxes. (Online dictionary).

In the latter case, the authorities are not established, they are just "wanna bes" (for lack of better terminology). Just about every job has them and it is okay to be disobedient to them if they approach you disrespectfully.

#56

Do you have an attitude of gratitude?

Ruth 2:10:

> *Then she fell on her face, and bowed herself to the ground, and said unto him, Why have I found grace in thine eyes, that thou shouldest take knowledge of me, seeing I am a stranger?*
>
> (King James Version)

*R*uth in this text, had an attitude of gratitude. Unlike Vashti, (See Esther chapter 1) who, because she was pretty to look at, became conceited and just like Lucifer, iniquity was found in her. She began to think that her beauty entitled her to be queen, but she was in for a rude awakening when she lost her status due to her disobedience, which was rooted in her pride. The opposite of gratitude is entitlement. An entitlement is a right, but the problem is that rights have the tendency to infuse or instill pride in a person, just as responsibilities have the tendency to infuse or instill humility.

One must be careful with one's attitudes and actions when it comes to rights.

#57

Do you have a hard time acknowledging mistakes?

Jeremiah 3:13:

> *Only acknowledge thine iniquity, that thou hast transgressed against the LORD thy God, and hast scattered thy ways to the strangers under every green tree, and ye have not obeyed my voice, saith the LORD.* (Good News Translation)

Only acknowledge, saith the Lord. To acknowledge is to admit to a fact being real or true; to recognize the existence of a thing. The Lord wants us to acknowledge our mistakes and sins when we are wrong, but the spirit of pride says the self is above mistakes. 1 John 1:8-9 says **If we say that we have no sin, we deceive ourselves, and there is no truth in us. ⁹But if we confess our sins to God, he will keep his promise and do what is right: he will forgive us our sins and purify us from all our wrongdoing.** (Good News Translation). Pride makes it difficult for one to acknowledge mistakes. This is why God resists the proud but gives grace to the humble (see James 4:6).

#58

Retaliation

Romans 12:17-19:

*Recompense to no man evil for evil. Provide
things honest in the sight of all men. If it be
possible, as much as lieth in you, live peace-
ably with all men. Dearly beloved, avenge not
yourselves, but rather give place unto wrath:
for it is written, vengeance is mine; I will repay
saith the Lord*

$\mathcal{R}$etaliation is you striving for gratification of your frustration. Someone has hurt you or done something you
do not like. You are frustrated with them and so you want your
frustration gratified. However, the only way your frustration
will get gratified is if the person you are aiming at, shows vis-
ible signs of their frustration with what you have done. Because
if after you retaliate, the person shows no sign of frustration,
in fact they completely ignore you, then your frustration gets
worse. However, God is telling us not to repay evil for evil,
especially to those who are of the household of faith. The spirit
of pride wants to retaliate at all cost.

Why does God want us to leave vengeance to Him? Because He is just and fair even in anger, but we are not. When we are mad, we want the punishment to exceed the crime. This is the spirit of pride at work.

#59

Do you Want to get the last Word in an Argument?

Proverbs 29:11:

A fool uttereth all his mind: but a wise man keepeth it in till afterwards (King James Version)

*D*o you often feel like you must get the last word in an argument? So you can feel like you won the argument. Sometimes as Mike Murdock says: "the kindest word spoken, is an unkind word unsaid." Sometimes silence speaks louder than speech. According to this scripture, it is not everything that comes to our mind that we need to speak. We need "spiritual filters" to filter out the harmful and hurtful words.

60

Are the Purposes of God pretended while the purposes of Self are intended?

John 12:3-6:

> *³ Then Mary took about a pint[a] of pure nard, an expensive perfume; she poured it on Jesus' feet and wiped his feet with her hair. And the house was filled with the fragrance of the perfume.⁴ But one of his disciples, Judas Iscariot, who was later to betray him, objected, ⁵ "Why wasn't this perfume sold and the money given to the poor? It was worth a year's wages.[b]" ⁶ He did not say this because he cared about the poor but because he was a thief; as keeper of the money bag, he used to help himself to what was put into it.* (New International Version)

Judas did not really care for the poor, which would be the purposes of God (see Proverbs 19:17). He was really thinking about his purposes. The scripture says he was a thief and as treasurer of Jesus ministry, he used to steal from the money bag. So in his mind, rather than Mary honoring Jesus with it, the ointment should be sold and the money put in Jesus's ministry where he could greatly help himself to what was put into the money bag. We must constantly evaluate and examine our motivations for our actions, because for God, what you do is not as important as why you do it. What you do is outward and for man, but why you do it is of the heart (the spirit of man). Its inward and for God.

1 Samuel 16:7 says **But the LORD said to Samuel, "Do not consider his appearance or his height, for I have rejected him. The LORD does not look at the things people look at. People look at the outward appearance, but the LORD looks at the heart."** (New International Version).

#61

Praying Aloud in the Spirit
in a Public Gathering

1 Corinthians 14:18-19:

¹⁸ I thank God that I speak in tongues more than all of you. ¹⁹ But in the church I would rather speak five intelligible words to instruct others than ten thousand words in a tongue.

(New International Version)

*I*n many Charismatic, Pentecostal, COGIC (Church of God in Christ), nondenominational style churches, it is common to hear praying in the Spirit going on publicly in service. Praying in the Spirit is not to be confused with the gift of speaking in tongues which **ALWAYS** is accompanied by the corresponding interpretation of tongues so that the whole body can be edified (see 1 Corinthians 12). The bottom line is when the congregation is together, then edification (or the building up) of the whole congregation takes precedence to edification of self. When you pray in the Spirit you build up yourself (see Jude 1:20), but your neighbor who may not even be a believer

99

is not edified. Again, pride puts the need of the self above the need of others. Love does just the opposite: it puts others needs above the needs of self. Evidently, Paul was dealing with the same issue back then. Let your need to look "super deep" or your need to edify yourself be less important than your need to see that your neighbor, fellow congregant or visitor gets edified when you are in a public gathering such as service.

#62

Do you elevate your opinion to factual status?

Matthew 15:3:

> *But he answered and said unto them, Why do ye also transgress the commandment of God by your tradition?* (King James Version)

The Scribes and the Pharisees were guilty of elevating their opinions to traditions and factual status. They even elevated their traditions above God's commandments. They would not endure any opposition to their opinions, traditions and actions even if they were wrong. This is a clear manifestation of pride. We are not right all the time, neither do we have all knowledge. So, for us to take a position and refuse, to relinquish it despite the truth, is prideful.

When one elevates their opinion to factual status, they have become the originator, determinant and source of all moral good. They have become what Mark Pestana calls the moral subjectivist. All pride is moral subjectivism. God is the originator and the supreme being for all good. The moral subjectivist has turned away from God and established him/herself as the originator of all good.

#63

Forgetting the Lord

Deuteronomy 8:10-14:

> *¹⁰ You will have all you want to eat, and you will give thanks to the LORD your God for the fertile land that he has given you.¹¹ "Make certain that you do not forget the LORD your God; do not fail to obey any of his laws that I am giving you today. ¹² When you have all you want to eat and have built good houses to live in ¹³ and when your cattle and sheep, your silver and gold, and all your other possessions have increased, ¹⁴ be sure that you do not become proud and forget the LORD your God who rescued you from Egypt, where you were slaves.* (Good News Translation)

*P*rosperity breeds pride, which breeds amnesia or forgetfulness. When life is good, and things are going our way, we can become prideful (lifting of the heart) and forget God, who is the reason for the prosperity and that manifests itself in the way we treat or view our neighbor who maybe less fortunate than we have become. We forget that we too were once in our neighbors' shoes of poverty and lack. We start to look at our neighbors with disdain. This is the spirit of pride at work.

#64

Oppression of the Poor

Psalms 10:2-6:

The wicked are proud and persecute the poor;
catch them in the traps they have made.
(Good News Translation)

*A*ny form of oppression of the poor is a manifestation of pride. To oppress is to burden with cruel or
unjust impositions. Subject to a harsh exercise of authority or
power. Pride goes right along with violence. Violence can take
the form of oppression, discrimination, disenfranchisement,
exploitation, marginalization and many other forms of injustice.
When we think of violence and oppression, our minds tend to
go to shootings, lynching's etc., which they are, but it takes very
little to be oppressive and violent. For example, defamation of
character is violence and oppression against the neighbor.

It was Dr. Cornell West that said: "justice is what love looks
like in public" and that is so true. Now if justice is what love
looks like in public, and pride is the antithesis of love, then it
follows that injustice is what pride looks like in public. This
why scripture uses terms like love, just, no respecter of persons

to describe God (see 1 Corinthians 13, Romans 2, and Psalms 140 for references).

Psalms 25:9 says: **He leads the humble in justice, And He teaches the humble His way.** (New American Standard Bible). If God guides the humble in justice, then it follows that in matters of injustice and pride, He is not the guide, but rather, He opposes and resists the proud in matters of injustice. Furthermore, it is the self, the ego, the spirit of pride that is the guide in matters of injustice.

#65

Are you harder on others than you are on yourself?

Romans 2:1:

> *You, therefore, have no excuse, you who pass judgment on someone else, for at whatever point you judge another, you are condemning yourself, because you who pass judgment do the same things.* (New International Version)

The spirit of pride judges others harder than it does the self. It is tougher on others while it gives the self a pass or a break. However, according to Philippians 2:3, we are supposed to esteem others above ourselves or better than ourselves. We are to do to others as we would have them do to us (see Matthew 7:12).

#66

Gossip

1 Peter 4:15:

But let none of you suffer as a murderer, or as a thief, or as an evildoer, or as a busybody in other men's matters. (King James Version)

$\mathcal{G}$ossip is informal conversation about other people's private affairs. It usually involves some slander, defamation of character, rumors etc., the bible calls this being a busybody in other men's matters. The key is that it is the affairs, issues and mistakes of others that is being discussed. All the while, the affairs of the self (i.e., the gossipers affairs) are swept under the rug. Most times, those doing the gossiping, are not able to repeat what they said in the absence of the person, if or when the person is present.

#67

Do you cover your sins rather than confess them?

Proverbs 28:13:

He that covereth his sins shall not prosper: but whoso confesseth and forsaketh them shall have mercy. (King James Version)

The spirit of pride covers the sins of the self, while confessing the sins of others. However, covering a sin keeps one in bondage to it. The Kingdom of Darkness thrives in secrecy. Notice the scripture says confess and forsake (in that order). Until the sin is confessed it cannot be completely forsaken. One may be able to forsake for while without confession, but sooner or later then can easily fall back into it because the "backdoor was left open.

#68

Are you offended at the truth of God's word?

John 6:60-61:

> *⁶⁰ Many therefore of his disciples, when they had heard this, said, This is an hard saying; who can hear it?⁶¹ When Jesus knew in himself that his disciples murmured at it, he said unto them, Doth this offend you?* (King James Version)

Truth is progressive and manifold. There are levels of truth that the self cannot handle. Such was the case in this passage of scripture. Jesus the Word was speaking truth to His disciples, but they could not handle that level of truth. So, they said this is a hard saying, in other words, this is a difficult, harsh and offensive statement. Who can be expected to listen to it as the Amplified bible puts it. However, the truth is that it was not the saying that was hard, but rather, it was their hearts that was hard, which was due to their pride. It was taboo for Jesus to speak such a thing.

In the church today, there are taboos and truths that people get offended at if preached about from the pulpit. For example, sex, homosexuality, politics etc., but all these things are in the Word of God and if it be in the Word of God, then it is truth and it was put there for our learning and instruction. Romans 15:4 says: **Everything written in the Scriptures was written to teach us, in order that we might have hope through the patience and encouragement which the Scriptures give us** (Good News Translation).

So many churches do not teach or preach on subjects that are taboo even though the congregation may be plagues with the issue. If it be taught, one risks losing members and so in order to keep members, one may stay away from certain topics. In verse 66 of the same passage of scripture, Jesus lost some disciples, the bible says from that day on, many disciples turned back from following Him. There is an African proverb that says: truth has no friends. There is no truth higher than the Word of God. We should not water down or lower the standard of the Word, but rather pray to come up to its standards.

#69

Rebellion

1 Samuel 15:23:

for rebellion is as the sin of witchcraft and stub-
bornness is as iniquity and idolatry. Because
thou has rejected the word of the Lord, he hath
also rejected thee from being king.

(King James Version)

*I*f I went up to somebody (a believer) and said, do you
sometimes or occasionally practice witchcraft? They
might get offended at the question. However, scripture says that
there is no difference between rebellion, which is the Hebrew
word for sin, and witchcraft.

#70

Adultery

Ezekiel 23:37:

*They have committed adultery and murder—
adultery with idols and murder of the children
they bore me. They sacrificed my children to
their idols.* (Good News Translation)

Symbolically speaking, sexual intercourse represents worship. This is why when the children of Israel worshipped other gods (idols), it was called adultery. The worship that rightfully belongs to God has been given to someone or something else.

Hebrews 13:4 says: **Marriage is to be honored by all, and husbands and wives must be faithful to each other. God will judge those who are immoral and those who commit adultery.** (Good News Translation). Sex is to be done in the context of marriage. When it occurs in the context of marriage, God receives that as worship. However, when done outside the context of marriage then the spirit of pride is at work. The bible refers to the wife as the weaker vessel, just as in our relationship to Christ our head, we (the bride) are the weaker vessel.

The weaker vessel gives worship to their head, husband or male. So here are the implications for the male choosing to engage in sex outside of marriage. The male has put himself in the position of God and is receiving direct worship from the female. This is worse than what Satan did to get thrown out of heaven.

For the female choosing to engage in sex outside of marriage, she (the weaker vessel) is giving direct worship to her god (male counterpart). Therefore, fornication, adultery and any other form of sex that occurs outside the boundaries of marriage is illegal worship and it is rooted in the spirit of pride.

#71

Road Rage

Proverbs 16:32:

He that is slow to anger is better than the mighty; and he that ruleth his spirit than he that taketh a city. (King James Version)

*R*oad rage is a fit of violent anger by the operator of an automobile and it is usually directed at and endangering other motorists. People have lost their lives in road rage incidents. Road rage is a manifestation of pride, because it's about one's impatience and anger, which are two previously identified manifestations of pride.

People honk back and forth at each other and say curse words at each other. The honking is rather unpleasant as I have been on the receiving end of one of them. Ephesians 4:27 talks about not given the devil a foothold, because the longer you stay angry, the more difficult it is to stop being angry and this type of anger does not display or bring about the righteousness of God (see James 1:20).

#72

Self-Righteous

Luke 7:39:

When the Pharisee saw this, he said to himself, "If this man really were a prophet, he would know who this woman is who is touching him; he would know what kind of sinful life she lives!" (Good News Translation)

Self-righteous people are convinced that they are right in their beliefs, attitudes, and behavior and that other people are wrong, even the Word of God. They are very intolerant of the opinions and behaviors of others. Simon the Pharisee had invited Jesus to a dinner. At the dinner, Mary, Lazarus's sister (see John 11:2), comes to Jesus and begins to worship Him at His feet. The self-righteous Pharisee, thinking he was right in his opinion and intolerant of Mary's actions, begins to look at Jesus with contempt. Jesus who knows all things, knew what Simon was thinking and used this situation as a teachable moment to correct the Pharisees deceptive thinking. It was customary for visitors to have their feet washed by their host. Simon had failed to do this for Jesus. Truth be told, that is where his focus should have been, but such is the spirit of pride: focuses on the faults of others, much to the negligence of the fault of the self.

Isaiah 64:6 lets us know that our righteousness is as filthy rags. In the Hebrew, that word means a woman's menstrual cloth. Self-righteousness is a manifestation of pride.

#73

Not Wanting to Ask for help when you need it

Matthew 7:7:

> **ask, and it shall be given unto you; seek and ye shall find; knock and it shall be opened unto you** (King James Version)

James 1:5:

> *if any of you lack wisdom, let him ask of God, that giveth to all men liberally, and upbraideth not; and it shall be given him.*
> (King James Version)

We live in a culture that empowers and encourages self-sufficiency and independence. However, for believers, we need to realize that every step towards independence is a step away from God. We are kingdom citizens and, in a kingdom, we depend on the King for help. Being able to do things on our own is great, but those areas where we may struggle, we need to reach out for help rather than saying "I got it" or "I do not need any help."

#74

Self-Exaltation

2 Corinthians 10:18:

For it is not the one commending himself who is approved, but the one the Lord commends.
(Holman Christian Standard Bible)

To self-exalt is to praise, to extol, to raise oneself in rank, honor, power, position etc., but Jesus said in Luke 14:11: **For everyone who exalts himself will be humbled, and the one who humbles himself will be exalted."** (Holman Christian Standard Bible). It is not who commends themselves, or praises themselves that is approved, but the one the Lord praises. The Lord said of Job, have you considered my servant Job. Job did not say that about himself, but rather the Lord did because he was approved by God.

#75

Selfish Ambition

Jermiah 45:5:

And seekest thou great things for thyself? seek them not: for, behold, I will bring evil upon all flesh, saith the LORD: but thy life will I give unto thee for a prey in all places whither thou goest. (King James Version)

Selfishness and pride, go hand in hand. To be selfish is to care only for your own interests, benefits and welfare to the exclusion of others. Pride puts the interest of the self above the interest of others.

Pride is self-worship. It was Muhammad Ali that said: "service to others is the rent we pay for our time here on earth." Serving and ministering to others is serving God. Only the things we do for God matter. In this passage of scripture, God is rebuking Baruch (Jeremiah's secretary) for his selfish ambition. He cared more about his own interests than the destruction of the temple, those destined to be exiled and the land. Baruch wanted to be exempt from any and all calamity, while the rest of Israel suffered one terrible fate after the other.

God in loving care, rebukes him for his pride driven selfish ambition, forgives him and then gives him comfort to alleviate his fear, because God the Almighty understands that Baruch's pride is driven by his fear of self-preservation.

In this verse, God has shown us the blueprint to dealing with pride. First, we rebuke, or reprove the person acting pridefully, but we do not stop there. We must go the extra mile of identifying their fear and seeing how we can alleviate that concern. **All pride is driven by fear of some sort.** Therefore, if we can identify the root cause of fear, our pride goes nowhere.

#76

Do you despise prophesies?

1 Thessalonians 5:20:

Despise not prophesyings. (King James Version)

To despise is to view with contempt, disdain, to have a low opinion, to scorn, to loathe and to have a distaste off.

By prophesying in this passage of scripture, it is meant either the foretelling of future events as in one of the manifestations of spiritual gifts or the preached word, or inspired message. One would not expect any believer to despise prophecies but since it is written there, then it means it does happen and it ought not to happen, therefore, we should not engage in it because it comes from the spirit of pride.

#77

Anxiety

1 Peter 5:7:

Casting all your care upon him; for he careth for you. (King James Version)

*A*ccording to the online dictionary, anxiety is a distress or uneasiness of mind caused by **fear** of danger or misfortune. All pride is driven by fear of some sort. (I cannot emphasize that point enough). As in the case with anxiety, it is the fear of misfortune, or danger. However, 1 Peter 5:7 lets know hat we do not have to be anxious for anything, we can simply cast all our care unto the Lord in humble dependence and trust in Him.

#78

Sarcasm

John 19:3:

And said, Hail, King of the Jews! and they smote him with their hands. (King James Version)

Sarcasm is harsh or bitter derision. It could be in speech or writing but it means the opposite of what it seems to say. It is insincere in that regard and the purpose is to mock or to insult someone. In this passage of scripture, the Roman soldiers were saying "hail, King of the Jews" but they really meant the opposite (scum of Jews for example), and they were ridiculing, mocking, and insulting Jesus.

This is the spirit of pride at work. Sarcasm is deceptive in nature and we know that our level of deception is equal to our level of pride.

#79

Do you like preeminence
or wanting to be in charge?

3 John 9-11:

> *⁹ I wrote a short letter to the church; but Diotrephes, who likes to be their leader, will not pay any attention to what I say. ¹⁰ When I come, then, I will bring up everything he has done: the terrible things he says about us and the lies he tells! But that is not enough for him; he will not receive the Christians when they come, and even stops those who want to receive them and tries to drive them out of the church!* (Good News Translation)

Colossians 1:17-19 says this about Christ: **And he is before all things, and by him all things consist.¹⁸ And he is the head of the body, the church: who is the beginning, the firstborn from the dead; that in all things he might have the preeminence.¹⁹ For it pleased the Father that in him should all fulness dwell** (King James Version).

Notice however, that Christ was given preeminence by the father. He (Christ) did not give Himself preeminence. Diotrephes, in 3 John 9-11 gave himself preeminence, which is self-exaltation, which is rooted in the spirit of pride. His subsequent actions are all manifestations of pride: slander, telling lies, refusing to listen, keeping others out of the church etc.

Ministers of Christ should not be known for wanting preeminence. Selfish ambition will breed malice against anyone that opposes it. Malice and ill-will will manifest themselves on the lips of such a person. The church belongs to God. He purchased it with the blood of His son. Pastors are the under shepherds and should not lord it over God's heritage as Diotrephes did. It is a bad thing to do no good, but it is worse to hinder others that would. This is the spirit of pride and arrogance at work.

#80

Do you kick others when they are down or do you lift them up?

2 Samuel 9:1-3:

> *And David said, Is there yet any that is left of the house of Saul, that I may shew him kindness for Jonathan's sake?[2] And there was of the house of Saul a servant whose name was Ziba. And when they had called him unto David, the king said unto him, Art thou Ziba? And he said, Thy servant is he.[3] And the king said, Is there not yet any of the house of Saul, that I may shew the kindness of God unto him? And Ziba said unto the king, Jonathan hath yet a son, which is lame on his feet.* (King James Version)

*D*avid had just taken over Saul's kingdom. Saul had been trying to kill David when he was alive. Now Saul was dead and so also was his son Jonathan. However, David still desired to show kindness to any member of Saul's family that may have been alive. Sure enough, Saul's grandson who was disabled was still around. He was down on his luck. He could not really provide for himself, and now his grandfather was dead, and his kingdom was gone. David could have said, is there any member of Saul's family yet remaining that I can kill or enslave, but no, David chose to lift Mephibosheth, who was Saul's lame grandson. That desire to show kindness and favor to an enemy, comes from a forgiving, meek and humble spirit.

#81

Do you feel like you don't need God?

Luke 12:20-21:

> *[20] But God said unto him, Thou fool, this night thy soul shall be required of thee: then whose shall those things be, which thou hast provided? [21] So is he that layeth up treasure for himself, and is not rich toward God.*

(King James Version)

The bible tells us that money answers all things (Ecclesiastes 10:19), the bible also tells us that money is a defense (Ecclesiastes 7:12) and that you cannot serve God and money (Luke 16:13). Prosperity breeds pride and arrogance. Prosperity causes a lifting up of the heart and a subsequent forgetfulness of God. The rich forget that it is God who gives ability to gain wealth (Deuteronomy 8:18) and that the earth is the lord's and the fullness thereof, the world and everyone in it (Psalms 24:1).

The uncertainty of life leaves no room for pride. No one knows tomorrow, and the bible tells us that our lives is like vapor (James 4:14). The rich fool in the parable, probably forgot all about God. He thought he was the on in complete control. He was in for a rude awakening. The scripture tells us that our life and times are in His hands (Psalms 31:15) and that it is better to say, if the Lord wills, we will do this or do that (James 4:15). The bottom line is that we are dependent on God, we need God and it is pride and foolishness that makes one think otherwise.

The richness that counts is the richness in what matters to God, and what matters to God is justice, winning souls, and ultimate kingdom advancement. Micah 6:8 says: **He hath shewed thee, O man, what is good; and what doth the LORD require of thee, but to do justly, and to love mercy, and to walk humbly with thy God?** (King James Version).

#82

Are you wise in your own eyes?

Proverbs 3:7:

Be not wise in thine own eyes: fear the LORD, and depart from evil. (King James Version)

To be conceited is a form of pride. it is to have an excessive favorable opinion of one's abilities, appearances, etc., how do we know when we are being excessively favorable to ourselves? We disregard any other person's abilities, and we consider them trivial. We also overlook or consider trivial, the places where we are weak.

To be wise in one's own eyes is to be conceited and Proverbs 3:7 says it is the opposite of the fear of the Lord, which is the beginning of true wisdom (Proverbs 9:10). The danger of conceitedness or being wise in one's eyes is that the bible tells us there is a way that seems right to a man but the end there of is destruction (Proverbs 14:12). The bible also tells us that the heart is deceitful above all things (Jeremiah 17:9). We set ourselves on the path of destruction, when we become wise in our own eyes and pride goes before destruction (Proverbs 16:18).

#83

I don't need a Pastor or a Teacher, I can study for myself

Jeremiah 3:15:

And I will give you pastors according to mine heart, which shall feed you with knowledge and understanding. (King James Version)

*Y*ou are either a sheep or a shepherd. If you are a sheep, then you need the covering of a shepherd. If you are a shepherd, then it means you have sheep or at least someone under your tutelage.

In our text above, God said He has given us Pastors according to His heart... Sometimes when imperfect vessels in authority make mistakes, members of the congregation may leave or depart from the faith because they are hurt. They choose not to be united with any other local congregation. This shows that ultimately, they were following the Pastor not Christ. But let God be true and every man a liar (Rom. 3:4), and we should not think the less of truth even if the vessel is not practicing what the vessel is preaching. The truth is the truth, even if it is coming out of the devil's mouth. Solomon was the wisest man who ever lived, and we read and make references to his proverbs or wise sayings. However, we know that Solomon worshipped idols, his heart departed from the Lord, and he did not practice what he was teaching, Yet we still use his proverbs.

Pastors, teachers, apostles etc., can make mistakes and so can you. It is a huge mistake to defect from the body and the faith because leadership hurt you. Pray for the leadership, if you need to go somewhere else, then do so, but do not just disconnect from the body of Christ, saying you will not go anywhere. This is the spirit of pride, which will eventually lead to your destruction. Any part of the human body disconnected from the body eventually withers and dies. It is the same with the body of Christ. It is just a matter of time.

#84

I do not have to go to Church, I can worship from home

Hebrews 10:25:

Not forsaking the assembling of ourselves together, as the manner of some is; but exhorting one another: and so much the more, as ye see the day approaching. (King James Version)

During this period of the pandemic, churches have had to change the way they do service. In order to be safe and keep the corona virus from spreading, many churches have services online for people to stay home and watch. However, before the pandemic, there were a lot of believers whose manner it was to stay home and watch services on television. They claim it was the same; it was *not* the same and it was coming from a place of pride. We are a body; we need each other for strength. Everybody matters and everybody has a gift that is needed in the body. Thank God for technology and technological advancement, but we do not need to make technology a god.

Consider this, in third world countries where majority of the population is poor, and technology is not as far advanced as it is here. The pandemic is done away with, No one is wearing masks and there are no cases of outbreaks. Why is that? (a rhetorical question).

#85

Do you feel like the rules do not apply to you?

2 Chronicles 26:14-21:

[14] And Uzziah prepared for them throughout all the host shields, and spears, and helmets, and habergeons, and bows, and slings to cast stones. [15] And he made in Jerusalem engines, invented by cunning men, to be on the towers and upon the bulwarks, to shoot arrows and great stones withal. And his name spread far abroad; for he was marvellously helped, till he was strong. [16] But when he was strong, his heart was lifted up to his destruction: for he transgressed against the LORD his God, and went into the temple of the LORD to burn incense upon the altar of incense. [17] And Azariah the priest went in after him, and with him fourscore priests of the LORD, that were valiant men: [18] And they withstood Uzziah the king, and said unto him, It appertaineth not unto thee, Uzziah, to burn

incense unto the LORD, but to the priests the sons of Aaron, that are consecrated to burn incense: go out of the sanctuary; for thou hast trespassed; neither shall it be for thine honour from the LORD God.[19] Then Uzziah was wroth, and had a censer in his hand to burn incense: and while he was wroth with the priests, the leprosy even rose up in his forehead before the priests in the house of the LORD, from beside the incense altar.[20] And Azariah the chief priest, and all the priests, looked upon him, and, behold, he was leprous in his forehead, and they thrust him out from thence; yea, himself hasted also to go out, because the LORD had smitten him.[21] And Uzziah the king was a leper unto the day of his death, and dwelt in a several house, being a leper; for he was cut off from the house of the LORD: and Jotham his son was over the king's house, judging the people of the land.

(King James Version)

*T*he rule of law basically has the idea of no one being above the law. In other words, what's good for the Goose is good for the Gandy.

At PECO foods, all employees are required to wear a certain type of rubber steel-toed boots for safety. The United States Department of Agriculture (USDA) also has their employees at the plant inspecting and checking to see that every aspect of the production is in compliance with federal and state laws.

However, these USDA employees can wear whatever they want without repercussion. They come into the production area of the plant with sneakers and jewelry. Items that are unsafe for the production environment. If a PECO employee were to do that, they would be disciplined up to and including termination. They feel like the rules do not apply to them.

King Uzziah in this text was one who did not think that the rules applied to him because he was king. He knew that only the sons of Aaron were allowed to burn incense at the altar. It was a God-given ordinance, which he tried to bypass. He was able to withstand 80 priests, but he could not stand against the Lord, when he was struck with leprosy. The bible records that he died a leper in shame, when he should have died in glory.

#86

Discrimination/Prejudice

James 2:1-6:

My brethren, have not the faith of our Lord Jesus Christ, the Lord of glory, with respect of persons.² For if there come unto your assembly a man with a gold ring, in goodly apparel, and there come in also a poor man in vile raiment;³ And ye have respect to him that weareth the gay clothing, and say unto him, Sit thou here in a good place; and say to the poor, Stand thou there, or sit here under my footstool:⁴ Are ye not then partial in yourselves, and are become judges of evil thoughts?⁵ Hearken, my beloved brethren, Hath not God chosen the poor of this world rich in faith, and heirs of the kingdom which he hath promised to them that love him?⁶ But ye have despised the poor. Do not rich men oppress you, and draw you before the judgment seats? (King James Version)

*I*n the kingdom community, there should be no discrimination, partiality, prejudice, marginalization, or disenfranchisement based on status, wealth or any other category used to discriminate.

In the blueprint that Jesus gave His disciples to use when praying (see Matthew 6), He told them to begin by saying "Our Father." This means when we all come to God, He is our father, and we are His children, which makes all of us siblings. Whether we are the president of a country or we are in prison or homeless, when we come before God, we are equal and the ground is level.

Discrimination does not come from divine law. It comes from self-serving motives, which is a manifestation of pride.

#87

Do you want Autonomy or Accountability?

Matthew 25:14-28:

[14] For the kingdom of heaven is as a man travelling into a far country, who called his own servants, and delivered unto them his goods. [15] And unto one he gave five talents, to another two, and to another one; to every man according to his several ability; and straightway took his journey. [16] Then he that had received the five talents went and traded with the same, and made them other five talents. [17] And likewise he that had received two, he also gained other two. [18] But he that had received one went and digged in the earth, and hid his lord's money. [19] After a long time the lord of those servants cometh, and reckoneth with them. [20] And so he that had received five talents came and brought other five talents, saying, Lord, thou deliveredst unto me five talents: behold, I have gained beside

them five talents more.[21] *His lord said unto him, Well done, thou good and faithful servant: thou hast been faithful over a few things, I will make thee ruler over many things: enter thou into the joy of thy lord.*[22] *He also that had received two talents came and said, Lord, thou deliveredst unto me two talents: behold, I have gained two other talents beside them.*[23] *His lord said unto him, Well done, good and faithful servant; thou hast been faithful over a few things, I will make thee ruler over many things: enter thou into the joy of thy lord.*[24] *Then he which had received the one talent came and said, Lord, I knew thee that thou art an hard man, reaping where thou hast not sown, and gathering where thou hast not strawed:*[25] *And I was afraid, and went and hid thy talent in the earth: lo, there thou hast that is thine.*[26] *His lord answered and said unto him, Thou wicked and slothful servant, thou knewest that I reap where I sowed not, and gather where I have not strawed:*[27] *Thou oughtest therefore to have put my money to the exchangers, and then at my coming I should have received mine own with usury.*[28] *Take therefore the talent from him, and give it unto him which hath ten talents.* (King James Version)

*A*ccountability is the opposite of autonomy. Autonomy means independence, self-governed, doing whatever one wants whenever one likes. The danger with this however, is that as identified earlier, the heart is deceitful above all things (see Jeremiah 17:9) and there is a way that seems right but the end thereof is death (see Proverbs 14:12).

However, from this parable being told by Jesus, the Kingdom of God is a Kingdom of accountability. To be accountable is to be answerable. Therefore, accountability is connected to stewardship and stewardship responsibilities. The spirit of pride wants to be autonomous. We are all accountable to God and to each other. We are accountable for our time, talent and treasure. We are accountable for our relationships. Life is about accounting. There is coming a time, just like in the parable, when we have to answer and give an account of our stewardship.

Refusing to be accountable to anyone is a manifestation of pride. You want to be able to do what you want, when you want, and you do not want anyone telling you what to do, and what not to do. This is the spirit of pride at work.

#88

Greed

Colossians 3:5:

You must put to death, then, the earthly desires at work in you, such as sexual immorality, indecency, lust, evil passions, and greed (for greed is a form of idolatry). (Good News Translation)

Greed is the inordinate desire to have more of something (such as food or money) than is necessary or fair. When it comes to greed, one is willing to do anything to acquire more, even if it means exploiting the next person.

We are to have self-control (discipline), self-restraint and self-denial. Greed is the opposite of Godliness. Godliness with contentment is great gain and we are to be content with such things as we have (see 1Timothy 6:6 and Philippians 4:11). Greed says, Lord, you have not given me enough, so I am going to get more and more even if it means inconveniencing others. Greed says, Lord, my lust for the worldly things is stronger than my love for you.

On a brief study of the 10 commandments, one can notice that the first one (no other god…) is the most important in the relationship between God and man and the last one (thou shalt not covet) is the most important in our relationship with one another. Covetousness is greed. It is the ultimate destruction of neighborhood. The more I acquire and consume goods and commodities, the number I become towards the welfare of my neighbor. Particularly the vulnerable in society. The vulnerable in society are those with unprotected rights. In their culture back then, it was the widow, the orphan, and the alien. In our culture today, it would be aliens, felons, and sex offenders.

I highly recommend one reads Walter Brueggemann's book on Sabbath and saying no to the culture of now.

#89

Are you easily offended or provoked?

Proverbs 16:32:

He that is slow to anger is better than the mighty; and he that ruleth his spirit than he that taketh a city. (King James Version)

The bible tells us that God is slow to anger and quick to mercy. It follows that if a person is quick to anger, that person will be slow to mercy. Getting offended easily, means one is impatient and intolerant of other people's mistakes. These are manifestations of pride. Being quick to anger means sweating and fretting the small things., which means you overlook the big things. In Matthew 23:25-26, Jesus said to the Pharisees you strain out a gnat and swallow a camel! It cannot be said any better than that. The things and situations the Pharisees should have been angry at, they were not, but the little insignificant situations, they were furious and vexed about.

When we are quick to anger, the devil can take over or gain ground on us. If you let the sun, go down on your wrath, then you are staying angry too long and consequently, you are giving Satan place to steal, kill and destroy you. (see John 10:10)

#90

Do you magnify offenses done to you while minimizing offenses you do to others?

Matthew 18:23-35:

²³ Therefore is the kingdom of heaven likened unto a certain king, which would take account of his servants.²⁴ And when he had begun to reckon, one was brought unto him, which owed him ten thousand talents.²⁵ But forasmuch as he had not to pay, his lord commanded him to be sold, and his wife, and children, and all that he had, and payment to be made.²⁶ The servant therefore fell down, and worshipped him, saying, Lord, have patience with me, and I will pay thee all.²⁷ Then the lord of that servant was moved with compassion, and loosed him, and forgave him the debt.²⁸ But the same servant went out, and found one of his fellowservants, which owed him an hundred pence: and he laid hands on him, and took him by

the throat, saying, Pay me that thou owest.[29]
And his fellowservant fell down at his feet, and
besought him, saying, Have patience with me,
and I will pay thee all.[30] *And he would not: but*
went and cast him into prison, till he should
pay the debt.[31] *So when his fellowservants saw*
what was done, they were very sorry, and came
and told unto their lord all that was done.[32]
Then his lord, after that he had called him,
said unto him, O thou wicked servant, I for-
gave thee all that debt, because thou desiredst
me.[33] *Shouldest not thou also have had com-*
passion on thy fellowservant, even as I had
pity on thee?[34] *And his lord was wroth, and*
delivered him to the tormentors, till he should
pay all that was due unto him.[35] *So likewise*
shall my heavenly Father do also unto you, if
ye from your hearts forgive not every one his
brother their trespasses. (King James Version)

Sin is an offense, and an offense is a debt. Victims tend to magnify (exaggerate) the significance or effect of the offenses done to them, because it gives more justification for control, which equals power: "you owe me" …, but this is the spirit of pride. It is also the spirit of pride to minimize the significance or effect of an offense one has done (Perpetrator) to others. They may say things like: "I only did this," or "it was just" … the perpetrator is trying to hold on to some power (Control).

However, when we magnify offenses done to us, we hold on to grudges, while we forget or we fail to realize **that no matter what the magnitude of the offense done to us is, it**

pales in comparison to the magnitude of offense we have done to God.

In the parable of the unforgiving servant, the unforgiving servant forgot or failed to realize that the magnitude of the offense done to him by his fellow servant, paled in comparison to the magnitude of offense he had done to the Master. Therefore, the places in our lives where we are God-oriented, we will be humble but the places in our lives where we ae self-oriented, we will be prideful.

#91

Do you not attend services because you have "nothing to wear"?

Luke 11:39:

> *So the Lord said to him, "Now then, you Pharisees clean the outside of your cup and plate, but inside you are full of violence and evil.* (Good News Translation)

*A*gain, these are pandemic times and churches have switched to online services. However, before the pandemic, there were people who would say they were not going to attend church because they had nothing to wear i.e., no church clothes or Sunday's best. This is the spirit of pride. However, just like Jesus was saying to the Pharisees, the inside of the cup is more important than the outside of the cup. In the same way, it is the heart of a man that is more important than the house (body or temple). Now, would we all like to wear our Sunday's best and look nice? Yes, but it should not take priority over our assembling together (see Hebrews 10:25). We should not be more concerned about how we look on the outside than how we look on the inside. **How we look on the outside is for man, but how we look on the inside, is for God.** (See 1Samuel 16:7).

#92

Slander

Psalms 31:13:

*For I have heard the slander of many: fear was
on every side: while they took counsel together
against me, they devised to take away my life.*
(King James Version)

Slander is untrue an defamatory statement or report about
someone with the purpose of damaging their reputation.
The United States presidential debate, as well as other polit-
ical debates, usually degenerate into slander. However, slander
is a manifestation of pride. Ephesians 4:29 says, **let no corrupt communication proceed from your mouth....** Two
adults should be able to have a debate and argument without
it degenerating into attacks on the other person's character or
reputation. Slander is based on the opinion of the one doing the
slandering. The slanderer has elevated their opinion to factual
status, which is another manifestation of pride. We must put
ourselves in the shoes of the other person. If someone said this
to me, how would I feel? If you would not like it, then probably
they would not like it as well, so it shouldn't be done.

#93

Do you change the truth of God's word into a lie?

Romans 1:25-30:

²⁵ Who changed the truth of God into a lie, and worshipped and served the creature more than the Creator, who is blessed for ever. Amen.²⁶ For this cause God gave them up unto vile affections: for even their women did change the natural use into that which is against nature:²⁷ And likewise also the men, leaving the natural use of the woman, burned in their lust one toward another; men with men working that which is unseemly, and receiving in themselves that recompence of their error which was meet.²⁸ And even as they did not like to retain God in their knowledge, God gave them over to a reprobate mind, to do those things which are not convenient;²⁹ Being filled with all unrighteousness, fornication, wickedness, covetousness, maliciousness; full of

envy, murder, debate, deceit, malignity; whis-
perers,[30] Backbiters, haters of God, despiteful,
proud, boasters, inventors of evil things, dis-
obedient to parents, (King James Version)

*C*hanging the truth of God's word into a lie, is a mani-festation of pride. This is a work of iniquity. There is a difference between missing the mark or falling short and deliberate and intentional practice of iniquity. When we practice something, we hope to get better at it. The people that the scripture is referring to in this passage of scripture, practice changing the truth of God's word into a lie and they hope to get better at doing it. This is the spirit of pride and idolatry at work. Believers may sin but they do not practice changing the truth of God's word into a lie.

#94

Stealing

Exodus 20:15:

Thou shalt not steal. (King James Version)

Stealing is idolatry. When we steal, we take something we do not have the right to take. In other words, we do so presumptuously, and presumption is the crime of idolatry. John 10:10 says: **The thief cometh not, but for to steal, and to kill, and to destroy: I am come that they might have life, and that they might have it more abundantly.** (King James Version)

Just as stealing is idolatry, killing is also idolatry. When we take a life, we take something we do not have the right to take. We are not the giver of life, so we do not have the right to take it. When one has the legal right, then one is authorized, but when one does not have the legal right, then that is idolatry. In other words, **idolatry is the opposite of authority.**

#95

Do you go on the defensive when challenged or questioned?

Genesis 4:9:

> *And the LORD said unto Cain, Where is Abel thy brother? And he said, I know not: Am I my brother's keeper?* (King James Version)

*I*n this passage of scripture, Cain went on the defensive when questioned by God about his brother. First, he lied and then he went on the defensive. Lying is a manifestation of pride and so is going on the defensive. He went on the defensive to cover his lie and ultimately his pride. Lying is going on the defensive. He knew his brother was dead, and that he was the one responsible for his death. If he really did not know where his brother was, he might have said he did not know and left it at that. Rather he chose to ask God the question as if to say, are you not my brother's keeper? You are the almighty God.

However, when God asks us questions, He is not asking because He does not know the answer, but rather He is giving us an opportunity to confess and come clean. Justification before God happens through the avenue of confession so that He can be found to be true and we a lie. For the scripture says let God be true and every man be a liar.

#96

Are you poor in spirit?

Matthew 5:3:

***Blessed are the poor in spirit: for theirs is the
kingdom of heaven.*** (King James Version)

There are many explanations on this verse as to who are
the poor in spirit. All explanations are good and could fit,
as the scripture says we know in part (see 1 Corinthians 13:9-
12). One thing we can all agree on though, is that the **poor in
spirit are not the proud in spirit.**

I see the poor in spirit as those who patiently and consistently take on the burdens of others. Particularly when it comes
to offenses and forgiveness. When one forgives, they take on
the additional burden of the offender, thus letting the offender
off the hook. I have often heard preachers say you "free yourself" when you forgive, but forgiveness is the opposite of that:
when you forgive, you take on the additional burden of the
offender thereby letting the offender go free. Here is a rhetorical question to consider: when Jesus forgave us, did He go free
or did we go free?

The concept of forgiveness can be better understood using financial debt: Let us say we have an individual by the name of John who is rich. He loans a friend his apple computer, but the friend damages the computer. This computer costs $3000, but the friend does not have the $3000 to pay John for the computer. So, John graciously forgives the debt and lets his friend off the hook for the $3000. However, the computer is still damaged, and John still needs to pay $3000 to get it replaced. John will have to come out of pocket his pocket, another $3000.

Let us say John lends another friend, $10,000 to be paid back in 6 months, but after six months, the friend is unable to pay. So, John once again graciously forgives the $10,000 debt. Now this $10,000 was money John was to use to fix something in his house, which still needs fixing. John will have to come out of his pocket another $10,000.

If John continues to forgive debts in this manner, at some point, John who was once rich will become financially strapped or poor because he is taking on additional financial burdens of the offender when he forgives their debt.

It works the same way in the spirit. So, the poor in spirit are those who consistently and patiently take on the burdens of others. For example, burdens of guilt, pain, shame etc.

The proud in spirit would never forgive such debts. If John was proud in spirit, he would require the debt even when the friend was unable to pay. The debt would never be cancelled and will always be used against the friend.

Now let us say in the first example, the friend said to John, "I damaged your property, and here is the money for it" then that would not be forgiveness of debt, that would be justice. John and his friend would be even.

#97

Hardening of the heart

Hebrews 3:15:

*While it is said, To day if ye will hear his voice,
harden not your hearts, as in the provocation.*
(King James Version)

*H*ardening of the heart or "hardening of weakness" as some philosophers put it, is caused by pride. **Pride weakens the will.** Hardening of the heart occurs because the axiological orders of good and evil are present and while the moral realist acknowledges God as the supreme originator and source of all good, the moral subjectivist (prideful spirit) has made him/herself originator or source of what is deemed good or valuable. However, the frustration for this individual is that he or she is always aware of the truth or the reality of a higher good. This presents an internal conflict: do I continue to pursue what I deem is valuable or do I submit to a higher source of good? This internal conflict rages especially for believers who have knowledge of the truth. For the individual, (who knows they need to make a change and abandon their pursuit but cannot do so because the will is weak) to put to rest the internal conflict, they must harden their heart, block out the truth completely and commit totally to their own pursuit, which ultimately ends in self-destruction.

Every decision to continue pursuit of what the individual deems to be valuable or good, further weakens the will, and since the individual has made up their mind to block out the truth, (by hardening their heart), then the individual has in a sense signed the self-destruction sheet.

However, in this passage of scripture, when one hears the voice of the Lord, one should yield and acknowledge because the alternative is to harden the heart, which ultimately ends in destruction.

#98

Martha Syndrome

Luke 10:38-42:

[38] Now it came to pass, as they went, that he entered into a certain village: and a certain woman named Martha received him into her house.[39] And she had a sister called Mary, which also sat at Jesus' feet, and heard his word.[40] But Martha was cumbered about much serving, and came to him, and said, Lord, dost thou not care that my sister hath left me to serve alone? bid her therefore that she help me.[41] And Jesus answered and said unto her, Martha, Martha, thou art careful and troubled about many things:[42] But one thing is needful: and Mary hath chosen that good part, which shall not be taken away from her. (King James Version)

The Martha syndrome is about our misplaced priorities and identifying our true motivations for doing ministry. Martha received Jesus and His disciples into her home. It was the custom of the Jews to wash the feet of their visitors and give them something to eat. Martha seeing how many feet she would have to wash and mouths to feed, became burdened. Furthermore, her sister Mary, did not offer to help, but rather went straight to sit at the feet of Christ to listen to His teaching. Martha's burden was exacerbated by her looking at what her sister was doing rather than focusing on the task. If her motivation was truly to serve Christ, then it mattered not what her sister was doing. She should have focused on serving cheerfully. Then God would have graced her to do it. She then goes to complain to Christ about her sister, expecting Christ to side with her in telling Mary to go and help, but Christ in fact rebukes her for her worry and anxiety (both of which are manifestations of pride).

There was a blessing for Mary, for choosing to sit at the Lord's feet. There would have been a blessing for Martha had she served cheerfully with the right motivation. Though she should be commended for entertaining Christ and His disciples, but she was obviously doing more than she could handle.

The Martha syndrome is also about this culture of work, work, work and more work without Sabbath (rest). One can imagine, that Martha and her sister Mary were probably working prior to Christ arrival. While Mary chose Sabbath (rest and trust in the Lord), Martha chose to continue working, which led her to be burdened by too much work.

#99

Interrupting someone while they are talking

Luke 18:35-43:

[35] As Jesus was coming near Jericho, there was a blind man sitting by the road, begging. [36] When he heard the crowd passing by, he asked, "What is this?"[37] "Jesus of Nazareth is passing by," they told him.[38] He cried out, "Jesus! Son of David! Have mercy on me!"[39] The people in front scolded him and told him to be quiet. But he shouted even more loudly, "Son of David! Have mercy on me!"[40] So Jesus stopped and ordered the blind man to be brought to him. When he came near, Jesus asked him, [41] "What do you want me to do for you?""Sir," he answered, "I want to see again."[42] Jesus said to him, "Then see! Your faith has made you well."[43] At once he was able to see, and he followed Jesus, giving thanks to God. When the crowd saw it, they all praised God. (Good News Translation)

$\mathcal{I}$nterrupting someone while they are speaking means cutting them off. It tells the person speaking that you do not care what they have to say. You think that your voice is more important, or you do not have time to listen to them.

This was certainly the case in this passage of scripture. The people in front of the blind man interrupted him to get him to keep quiet. They did not care that he was blind and trying to get his deliverance. They felt like his voice was not important, but good for him, because the more they tried to hush him, the louder he got. He eventually caught the attention of Jesus and received his deliverance.

#100

Bondage to sin

John 8:34:

Jesus said to them, "I am telling you the truth: everyone who sins is a slave of sin.

(Good News Translation)

2 Kings 5:11:

[11] But Naaman left in a rage, saying, "I thought that he would at least come out to me, pray to the LORD his God, wave his hand over the diseased spot,[a] and cure me! [12] Besides, aren't the rivers Abana and Pharpar, back in Damascus, better than any river in Israel? I could have washed in them and been cured!"[13] His servants went up to him and said, "Sir, if the prophet had told you to do something difficult, you would have done it. Now why can't you just wash yourself, as he said, and be cured?" [14] So Naaman went down to the Jordan, dipped himself in it seven times, as Elisha had instructed,

and he was completely cured. His flesh became firm and healthy like that of a child. (Good News Translation)

*J*esus said in John 8:34, that everyone who sins is a slave to sin. Our pride keeps us in bondage to sin, or addiction, or whatever vice we struggle with. In this passage of scripture, Naaman was a valiant warrior, but he had leprosy. Scripturally, leprosy represents sin. He was told to go and deep in the murky, and dirty Jordan river, in order to be rid of his disease. However, he became angry, and his pride would not let him do as he was told. It took the servants talking to him and him heeding their council to go back and do as the prophet Elisha had said. Had he not done that, he would have remained a leper. He felt dipping in the Jordan was beneath him. This is the spirit of pride that keeps us in bondage. The spirit of pride will also keep us from admitting that we need help to overcome addictions, or even acknowledge that we have an addiction. The spirit of pride will keep us in bondage to fear, anger, drugs, etc. Jesus came to deliver us from this bondage and the more we walk with Christ, the humbler we should be becoming. The more freedom of the will we should be experiencing.

We should take everyday opportunities to practice being humble. For example, say thank you more often and show appreciation for what others do for you, however little it may seem. Apologize or issue apologies more often. Ask questions you already know the answers to, because something may be said that you did not previously consider.

We need to watch for the spirit of pride from moment to moment, otherwise it will go unchecked and wreak havoc in our lives.

#101

Prodigality

Luke 15:11-32:

¹¹ And he said, "There was a man who had two sons. ¹² And the younger of them *said to his father, 'Father, give me the share of property that is coming to me.' And he divided his property between them. ¹³ Not many days later, the younger son gathered all he had and took a journey into a far country, and there he squandered his property in reckless living. ¹⁴ And when he had spent everything, a severe famine arose in that country, and he began to be in need. ¹⁵ So he went and hired himself out to[ª] one of the citizens of that country, who sent him into his fields to feed pigs. ¹⁶ And he was longing to be fed with the pods that the pigs ate, and no one gave him anything.*

¹⁷ "But when he came to himself, he said, 'How many of my father's hired servants have more than enough bread, but I perish here with hunger! [18] *I will arise and go to my father, and I will say to him, "Father, I have sinned against heaven and before you.* [19] *I am no longer worthy to be called your son. Treat me as one of your hired servants."'* [20] *And he arose and came to his father. But while he was still a long way off, his father saw him and felt compassion, and ran and embraced him and kissed him.* [21] *And the son said to him, 'Father, I have sinned against heaven and before you. I am no longer worthy to be called your son.'*[b]

[22] *But the father said to his servants,*[c] *'Bring quickly the best robe, and put it on him, and put a ring on his hand, and shoes on his feet.* [23] *And bring the fattened calf and kill it, and let us eat and celebrate.* [24] *For this my son was dead, and is alive again; he was lost, and is found.' And they began to celebrate.*

[25] *"Now his older son was in the field, and as he came and drew near to the house, he heard music and dancing.* [26] *And he called one of the servants and asked what these things meant.* [27] *And he said to him, 'Your brother has come, and your father has killed the fattened calf, because he has received him back safe and sound.'* [28] *But he was angry and refused to go in. His father came out and entreated him,* [29] *but he answered his father, 'Look, these many years I have served you, and I never disobeyed your command, yet you never gave me a young*

goat, that I might celebrate with my friends.
³⁰ But when this son of yours came, who has
devoured your property with prostitutes, you
killed the fattened calf for him!' ³¹ And he said
to him, 'Son, you are always with me, and all
that is mine is yours. ³² It was fitting to cele-
brate and be glad, for this your brother was
dead, and is alive; he was lost, and is found.'"

The word prodigal means waste or lavish. In this parable of the prodigal son, the father of the brothers is a picture of God the father. The prodigal son is a picture of anyone who is lost or in a backslidden state. I have often heard this parable being preached from the perspective of the father or from the perspective of the prodigal son. However, the truth is that the older brother who never left home was just as prodigal as the younger brother who did. He wasted his time, talents and opportunities. Notice he was with the father physically, but his heart was far away from the father's. His heart was lost and prodigal. His heart had shunted and worse still, he did not even know it. The father said son you are always with me (see verse 31) in other words, you have had access to all the resources, and you could have been celebrating and partying with your friends all this time.

Every step away from the father is a step away from wisdom and a step towards waste. In other words, **waste is the opposite of wisdom**. We know from Proverbs 11:2 that with the humble is wisdom. Therefore, it follows that if wisdom is with the humble, then waste is with the proud. Waste represents living for self rather than the purposes of God.

Prodigality is a manifestation of pride.

Closing Prayer

Pray this prayer after you have read this book:

$\mathcal{F}$ather, I thank you for revealing to me the areas of my pride that hinders Your grace in my life. Lord I repent right now and ask you to forgive me for my prideful ways. I ask you Holy Spirit of truth to help me and to give me the grace and strength to overcome in those areas In Jesus name I pray. Amen.

Author's Note

$\mathcal{A}$s devastating as the spirit of pride is to our human existence and our faith walk, it should be taught more and focused on more than it currently is in the body of Christ.

We will never be completely rid of the disease of pride on this side of eternity, but like any other disease, which one must deal with for the rest of one's life, careful monitoring of the disease can greatly minimize its destructive effects. Thus, one can thrive and survive while keeping the disease in check. For pride, there must be constant self-evaluation: moment to moment, hourly, daily etc.

Acknowledgements

I would like to acknowledge the following people, whom I call the faithful few:

Dr.Joseph Rukus (Rest in Love), thank you for your support and belief in what Future For Felons Inc. stands for. You were our most arduous supporter. I miss just being able to come by your office and pick your brain for ideas. You always had a lot of great ideas and insight for us. You used to say, I know my time is short, so I would like to make an impact before I live. Well, you made an impact in our lives and wherever Future For Felons Inc. is mentioned your name will be mentioned alongside.

Dr. Cherisse Jones-Branch, thank you for your love, dedication, unwavering support, and belief in Future For Felons Inc. and in me as a person. I say unwavering because whether I am up or down, at my worst or at my best, you never changed in your commitment to me or Future For Felons Inc. You are my most faithful investor, and I know that there are people who are naysayers, who would like for you to drop Future For Felons Inc., but nevertheless you remain loyal. You are a Godsend. The world needs more people like you. I remember one day while I was visiting with you in your office, you made the comment: "I don't think I have ever said No to you." I thank God for you, and I am so grateful for all you do. Thank you for your diligence, patience and intelligence. Thank you for your time, thank you for listening, for understanding, for your attention to details, for smiling and for your humor. Thank you for caring and for sharing and I know that your plate is full, and you are pulled in several directions. Yet you still make time to meet with me and for Future For Felons Inc. You are a shining example of the Proverbs 31 woman.

I want you to know that Future For Felons Inc. loves and appreciates you, and I love and appreciate you. I pray that God continues to bless you and your household. I pray that God continues to bless the work of your hands, that you continue to prosper and be in good health even as your soul prospers. I pray that God increases you in wisdom, and in strength. I pray that God continues to protect you as you drive on the highways, and that no weapon that is formed against you or your household prospers in the name of Jesus I pray.

More grease (power) to your elbows, keep up the good work and I am sure there are several other people and organizations echoing my sentiments.

Kerry Newcomb, thank you for going over and above the call of duty. Thank you for keeping me out of trouble both on and off the job. I remember when I told you I was writing a book, your first words to me were: "I can't wait to read it" that meant a lot to me and I would like to thank you for that.

Deacon Bernard Williams, thank you for always checking on me. I appreciate every random call and text. You had said if I wrote a book, you would love to read it, well here you go.

Maddie Vindiola, thank you for always believing in me and pushing me. You push me to bring out the best in me. You refuse to let me settle for less and I appreciate you for that. It takes a great leader to get the best out of everyone under the leader's care and you are an example of a great leader.

Sherry Manley, thank you for always greeting me with a smile. It makes my day. I cannot count how many times my day maybe going bad, and you walk by with a pleasant smile. It makes a huge difference. So, I say to you, keep on smiling.

CPSIA information can be obtained
at www.ICGtesting.com
Printed in the USA
LVHW021656070622
720712LV00020B/602